ALL THINGS NEW

ALL THINGS NEW

Lakeisha Goudy

ALL THINGS NEW

Copyright © 2024 Lakeisha Goudy

Published by Lakeisha Goudy
Sacramento, California U.S.A.

Unless otherwise noted, Scripture quotations are taken from the Holy Bible, New Living Translation. Copyright © 1996, 2004, 2007, 2013, 2015 by Tyndale House Foundation. Used by permission of Tyndale House Publishers, Inc., Carol Stream, Illinois 60188. All rights reserved.

Scripture quotations marked NKJV are from the New King James Version®. Copyright © 1982 by Thomas Nelson. Used by permission. All rights reserved.

Scripture quotations marked KJV are taken from the King James Version of the Bible. Public domain.

Cover Design: Lakeisha Goudy
Cover Photos: Giulia Vasta Photography

Library of Congress Control Number: 2024903694

ISBN: 979-8-9901149-0-6 (Paperback)

Printed in the United States of America

DEDICATION

I dedicate this book to my children, De'jon, Cameryn, and Cayden. I also dedicate this book to my little sister, Larissa. You guys inspire me to be better. I love you guys with all my heart. I hope this book inspires you to live a life that honors Jesus Christ.

"Therefore, if anyone is in Christ, he is a new creation; old things have passed away; behold, all things have become new."
(II Corinthians 5:17 NKJV)

Welcome to your new season of *All Things New!*
New blessings are on the way.

- Lakeisha Goudy

CONTENTS

ACKNOWLEDGMENTS

I want to thank God for all He has done in my life. Without Him, I do not know where I would be. Thank you for your love, grace, mercy, forgiveness, and correction. Thank you for giving me the wisdom and courage to write this book. Thank you for making *All Things New* in my life. Thank you for helping me build a legacy with you as the foundation. Thank you to my family for loving me, flaws and all. Thank you to everyone who has inspired, helped, encouraged, and shown me love throughout my journey. All of you are truly appreciated. Thank you to every person who will purchase and read this book. I pray it blesses you and leads you closer to Christ.

1

PURPOSE

What is your *purpose?* That is a question that everyone is searching for, even if they do not know it. Sadly, many people go to the grave unaware of their purpose. The only way to find your purpose is by seeking God. He is our Creator, and He knows the plans that He has for our lives. We seek purpose in material things, education, social status, finances, relationships, and achievements, but none of those things can fill the void of us not knowing our purpose.

God created us on purpose for a purpose. So we do not have to be confused about why we were created. We do not have to seek purpose in things of this world. The Bible says that *God knew us before He formed us in our mother's womb.* How powerful is that? He already had plans for our lives before we were formed in the womb, meaning we are here for a reason. We matter to God, and He wants great things for our lives. He loves us, and we are not a mistake. We are reverently and wonderfully made.

"Before I formed you in the womb I knew you; Before you were born, I sanctified you; I ordained you a prophet to the nations."
(Jeremiah 1:5 NKJV)

"I will praise You, for I am fearfully and wonderfully made; Marvelous are Your works, and that my soul knows very well."
(Psalms 139:14 NKJV)

This world hates God, and Satan has dominion over this world. His job is to steal, kill, and destroy. His goal is to destroy our lives and steal our purpose. Because of our lack of knowledge and us not truly having faith in God, we give Satan the authority to destroy our lives. We give him access to lead us away from God and His will for our lives.

"The thief does not come except to steal, and to kill, and to destroy. I have come that they may have life, and that they may have it more abundantly."
(John 10:10 NKJV)

We get so focused on our fleshly desires that we do not see how we are allowing Satan to steal our purpose and turn us away from God. Satan knows that by turning us away from God, we will never fulfill the plans that He has for our lives, we will never be set free from our sins, and we will live a life in bondage. I do not know about you guys, but I want to be set free. I want to receive everything that God has for me, and I want to walk in my purpose. Life is not just about our desires. We are here for so much more, and we must live like it.

We should chase after God as our lives depend on it. We need to allow Him to reveal our purpose and lead us as we fulfill it. We must let go of all the fleshly desires and things the world has instilled in us. We also must let go of all the negative things people have told us that make us feel unworthy of God's calling for our lives. *No matter what we think, God has created us for more than we can ever imagine. It's time for us to be set free from all the labels that Satan, society, trauma, and people have placed on us. It's time for us to live a life of purpose.*

"For we are God's masterpiece. He has created us anew in Christ Jesus, so we can do the good things he planned for us long ago."
(Ephesians 2:10 NLT)

MY TESTIMONY

I grew up with a lot of traumatic experiences, and it caused me to be confused about my purpose. I spent years of my life lost and trying to seek purpose in all the wrong things. In 2016, when I was going through a divorce, I decided I would put my faith in God and allow Him to lead me. I surrendered to God and let Him heal me and remove all the things that were not in His will for my life. I did not want to continue being led astray by the world or Satan. I was hungry for more. I wanted to know my purpose. I wanted to know what God saw in me because I knew how I viewed myself. The way I viewed myself was the opposite of how God saw me.

I grew up feeling like I was not good enough because I allowed people and circumstances to make me feel that way. No matter what I did throughout my life, the feeling of rejection would always come. That would lead me to believe nothing I did was ever good enough. Most of the rejection I felt came from those closest to me, such as family, people I thought were my friends and romantic relationships. Satan wanted that rejection to make me feel unworthy and unloved. He planted the seed, my experiences watered it, and instead of denying the lies, I believed them, and they grew.

I did not know it then, but some of that rejection was God trying to protect me. He was trying to protect me from people, places, and things unaligned with His will for my life. God knew everything He wanted for me, and He knew the woman I would eventually become. Even though I was not aligned with His word, He still had a calling for my life. He never gave up on me… Like He has a calling for my life, He has one for your life, too.

"For I know the plans I have for you," says the Lord. "They are plans for good and not for disaster, to give you a future and a hope." (Jeremiah 29:11 NLT)

When I gave my life to Christ, He instilled my purpose in me and showed me the type of woman He wanted me to be. Now, I do not have to seek validation from this world. I do not have to seek my purpose in people or things. I seek God for His plans for my life, and I let Him lead me. I do not focus on what the world says about who or what I should be. I focus on who God says I should be. Even if I must stand alone, I want His will for my life.

I truly hope this helps you begin to seek your purpose in God. Stop seeking it from people and things of this world. I hope you know you matter to God. The world needs you, and God is waiting for you to seek Him so that He can lead you to your calling. Don't let Satan steal your destiny. It's time to fight back against the attacks on your life. *It's time for you to come out from among them. It's time for you to walk in purpose.*

"Therefore, come out from among unbelievers, and separate yourselves from them, says the Lord. Don't touch their filthy things, and I will welcome you."
(2 Corinthians 6:17 NLT)

"And we know that all things work together for good to those who love God, to those who are the called according to His purpose."
(Romans 8:28 NKJV)

Purpose

How to Accept Jesus Christ:

1. Acknowledge that you are a sinner.

2. Pray and confess your sins to God.

3. Pray and ask Jesus to come into your heart.

4. Accept Him as Lord and Savior of your life.

The Prayer of Salvation

Dear Heavenly Father,

I come to You in the Name of Jesus Christ. Your Word says, *"Whosoever shall call on the name of the Lord shall be saved."* I call upon the name of Jesus Christ and ask that you come into my life and heart. I invite you to be the Lord of my life according to *Romans 10*, that if I openly declare that you are Lord and believe in my heart that God raised you from the dead, I will be saved. I believe in my heart that God raised you from the dead. I repent of my sins, and I surrender my life to you. I acknowledge and declare that you are the son of God. I believe and declare that you died on the cross for all of my sins and that you rose again on the third day. I believe in my heart and confess with my mouth that you are my Savior and Lord.
In the name of Jesus Christ,
Amen.

"If you openly declare that Jesus is Lord and believe in your heart that God raised him from the dead, you will be saved. For it is by believing in your heart that you are made right with God, and it is by openly declaring your faith that you are saved."
(Romans 10:9-10 NLT)

Take a few minutes to reflect and write down these things:

1. Write down things you tried to seek your purpose in.
   Pray and repent for seeking purpose in things of the world.

2. Write down lies and word curses spoken over your life by others.
   Rebuke and pray against those things.

3. Write down lies and word curses you spoke over yourself or believed about yourself.
   Renounce and repent for them.

4. Write down things God revealed about His plans and purpose for your life.
   Pray for His will over your life.

5. Write down scriptures that oppose the lies spoken over your life.
   Pray the scriptures over your life.

PRAYER

Dear Heavenly Father,

I repent for my sins and for the sins of my ancestors. I renounce and rebuke any demonic covenants and curses formed because of our lack of knowledge. We have not been obedient to your word. We have tried to seek purpose in everything but you. I ask for your forgiveness, grace, and mercy.

I repent for seeking my purpose in things of this world. I repent for allowing the voice of Satan and others to lead me away from you. I pray you instill my purpose in me. Reveal to me who I am in you. Help me see myself the way you see me.

Help me be a light to others and to use my testimony for your glory. I pray you block every demonic spirit trying to interfere with my purpose. I pray you give me the wisdom and knowledge to hear your voice above all voices. Help me not grow weary while I am walking in my calling. Help me seek you daily and die to my flesh.

Cleanse all the toxic thinking that the world has instilled in me. I want what you want for my life. I do not want to be aligned with anything that is not from you. I know your plans for me are greater than my plans. Redeem and restore any missed opportunities and wasted years I spent living against your will.

Cancel all demonic assignments on my life that are trying to delay my purpose and let the blood of Jesus Christ answer on my behalf. Re-establish my timeline to your divine appointed time. Lord, I forgive all the people who have tried to interfere with my purpose. I forgive myself for allowing deception to lead me astray. I forgive myself for not seeking you above this world.

I declare I am ready to accept the call you have for my life. I declare I am ready for this new season. I am prepared to walk in my purpose. I receive the purpose that you have for my life. Thank you for loving me. Thank you for your grace and mercy, even when I did not deserve it. Thank you for your protection. In the name of Jesus Christ, Amen.

Purpose

2

FAITH

Faith is something we must have if we want to live our lives as followers of Christ. The Bible says, *"Faith is the substance of things hoped for, the evidence of things not seen."* Even though we cannot see God, we can feel God's presence in our lives. If we cannot feel God's presence, our hearts are far from Him. The Bible also says, *"Without faith, it is impossible to please God."* If it's impossible to please God without faith, then there is no way around us not having faith in Him because we cannot please Him without faith.

"Now faith is the substance of things hoped for, the evidence of things not seen."
(Hebrews 11:1 NKJV)

"But without faith it is impossible to please Him, for he who comes to God must believe that He is, and that He is a rewarder of those who diligently seek Him."
(Hebrews 11:6 NKJV)

We put our faith in everything but God. We put our faith in people, jobs, finances, and even the government. We choose to trust people and things of this world over God. We cannot trust God without faith. We cannot receive the blessings of God without faith. We want God to bless us, but we do not trust Him. How can we expect God to move in our lives when we do not have faith in Him? We want God to answer our prayers, but *God moves in our lives according to our faith.*

In *Matthew*, Jesus healed two blind men. Before He healed them, He asked them if they believed He could heal them, and they believed He could. So, He told them, *"According to your faith, it is done."* They were healed instantly because they believed it could be done. That is just one example of healing being done according to faith. We need to believe so that it can and will be done according to our faith.

"When Jesus departed from there, two blind men followed Him, crying out and saying, "Son of David, have mercy on us!" And when He had come into the house, the blind men came to Him. And Jesus said to them, "Do you believe that I am able to do this?" They said to Him, "Yes, Lord." Then He touched their eyes, saying, "According to your faith let it be to you." And their eyes were opened. And Jesus sternly warned them, saying, "See that no one knows it." But when they had departed, they spread the news about Him in all that country."
(Matthew 9:27-31 NKJV)

Another thing that blocks us from having faith in God is *fear. Fear is a stronghold that Satan uses to get us out of God's will.* Once we are out of God's will, Satan has the authority to destroy our lives. Fear weakens us spiritually, mentally, emotionally, and physically. Fear opens the door for all kinds of demonic spirits to enter our lives, including premature death and illnesses. *We cannot have faith and fear at the same time.* One will always triumph over the other. *God does not give us a spirit of fear, nor does He want us to live in fear.* We must kill the spirit of fear as soon as it begins to form because if we do not, it will grow rapidly. We cannot afford to let fear stop us from trusting God. We cannot afford to let fear run our lives. *We must always choose faith over fear.*

"For God has not given us a spirit of fear, but of power and of love and of a sound mind."
(II Timothy 1:7 NKJV)

"Have I not commanded you? Be strong and of good courage; do not be afraid, nor be dismayed, for the Lord your God is with you wherever you go."
(Joshua 1:9 NKJV)

"The Lord is on my side; I will not fear. What can man do to me?"
(Psalms 118:6 NKJV)

In this season, we must learn to trust God and put our faith in Him. We cannot continue to waver regarding our faith in God. We do not have time to waste. The time is now. We must learn to trust God, no matter what it looks like. *We cannot let our circumstances control how we see God. We cannot continue to allow our trauma to interfere with how much faith we choose to put in God, and we cannot continue to allow how people treat us to affect our relationship with God.* We lose our faith in people, so we lose our faith in God. God is not fickle like us. God is not a man, that He should lie. *No matter what it looks like, we must trust God.*

"God is not a man, that He should lie, nor a son of man, that He should repent. Has He said, and will He not do? Or has He spoken, and will He not make it good?"
(Numbers 23:19 NKJV)

MY TESTIMONY

When I was going through my divorce over seven years ago, I was broken spiritually, emotionally, and mentally. I had no money saved, and after paying all my bills, I had about ten dollars to last for the month. I had not prepared for the storm that I was about to endure. I had to prepare to move out of my apartment because I knew I could not cover all my bills. Also, during that time, I did not know how to drive because I feared being in a car accident. My ex-husband did all the driving when we were together. So, after putting him out of our apartment, he kept the vehicle we both purchased together. So, during that time, my daughters and I had to catch the bus in the rain because my ex-husband did not want to help me.

I had only filed legal separation papers at the time because I was still torn on filing for a divorce, even though, in my heart, I knew our marriage was over. A part of me still wanted to hold on and believe that somehow, some way, my ex-husband would turn away from his sins, repent, and change. I thought he would realize that our family was worth fighting for and worth him changing for. I had fought for our marriage, and from my perspective, he never did. He made me the reason for all of his problems and never looked at the source of his problems. (himself) He assumed I would keep fighting for our marriage. I didn't...

Due to all of that, I was turning into someone I did not want to be. I was in unforgiveness, and because of that, a part of me wanted my ex-husband to feel the pain that he had caused me throughout our marriage. I did not curse, and I never wanted to, but during our marriage, when he would do hurtful things to me, I would curse him out. It was crazy because I would not curse any other time. I had let my relationship with him turn me into someone I did not want to be. I could feel my heart hardening over time, and even with all those feelings, I still loved him. I could feel that I was on the verge of a breakdown, and I had reached my breaking point. My heart was not aligned with God, and I had put my ex-husband as an idol in my life. I had put my marriage and things of the world above God. I had lost sight of what mattered. The thing that mattered to me was living a life that was pleasing to God. I truly wanted to honor God and live for Him.

I remember praying a lot during that time because I desperately needed God. I felt hopeless, and I wanted God's peace, healing, and love. I would pray to God about all the things my ex-husband did to me and was continuing to do to me. While praying, I heard God say, *"What about you?"* I remember thinking, *"What about me?"* *"He is the problem, and he needs to change."* Then I heard God say, *"You need to change, too."* In that season, He revealed that even though I was not doing everything, my ex-husband was doing, I was still living a life that was not pleasing to Him. I would read the bible and feel like I was being cut because of how powerful the words were. God was revealing to me in scripture what I needed to change, and it felt exactly like *Hebrews 4:12*. It did not feel good at the time being corrected by God, but it was needed. I wanted God to change my ex-husband, but God wanted to change me. He made me focus on my healing, so I did.

"For the word of God is alive and powerful. It is sharper than the sharpest two-edged sword, cutting between soul and spirit, between joint and marrow. It exposes our innermost thoughts and desires."
(Hebrews 4:12 NLT)

Within a few months, God gave me peace to file for divorce. Not only did God give me peace to end the marriage, but He also assured me that He would provide for my children and me. Even though I felt like I was lacking in almost every area, I decided to trust God, anyway. I took a leap of faith, no matter what my circumstances looked like. For the first time in my life, I fully trusted God.

God helped me overcome the fear of driving. I was able to buy a car and teach myself how to drive. I will never forget how proud of me my kids were. When they saw me driving, they clapped and said, *"Yay! Mommy knows how to drive now!"* I was shocked at how quickly I learned to drive because I had let fear steal that from me for years. Now, I know that it all happened quickly because God was restoring what Satan took from me. Not only did God restore it, but He also added speed to it. We must always remember that fear is not from God, and if we let fear control our lives, it will steal from us. I had let fear steal years of my life. At twenty-eight, I finally learned how to drive and got my license. I passed my written and driving tests on the first try. God even used my son's dad to help me get my license. He went with me to the DMV to take my Behind-The-Wheel Driving Test because you need someone who has car insurance and a valid driver's license to take the test. I had no one else to ask, so I was thankful that God used him to help me.

That year, God moved in my life more than I could have imagined. In August, I was officially divorced. Later that year, God used a pastor I know to find my children and me a place to stay. We moved in with a lady from church. We did not know each other, but moving in with her was a blessing. I genuinely appreciate her helping us in our time of need. God used various people in that season to assist me along the way.

I got a passport for the first time in November and went on my first Mission Trip to Mexico in December of that year. I did not know anyone in my family who had a passport or had gone on a Mission Trip. God knew He would use me in that season because of my *faith*. A few years earlier, I told myself that one day I wanted to go on a mission trip, and God brought it to pass. (I went on my second Mission Trip to the Philippines nine months later.)

At the beginning of that year, I was going through a horrible divorce; I did not know how to drive, I did not have a license, I was broke, I was heartbroken, I was in unforgiveness, and I was on the verge of a mental breakdown. I had just started to get aligned with God, but before the year was out, I was divorced, happy, and living for Christ. I had forgiven my ex-husband, as well as others who had hurt me. I had a driver's license, bought my first car on my own, had a new place to stay, had a passport, and went on my first Mission Trip. *God took my faith and blessed it with more than I could imagine.* If I had not stepped out on faith, I would have still been in a marriage that was not aligned with God and living a life that was not honoring God. Putting my faith in God changed everything in my life for the better.

I am beyond blessed and thankful for everything. I have been through a lot, but God has been with me. I have lost a lot, but I have gained so much more. I had to overlook my circumstances and trust

God. *We must put our faith in God, no matter what it looks like.* I trusted God in that season, which was one of the best things I ever did. I am not where I want to be, but I am not where I used to be. I know what it is like to live in fear. I lived in fear for a long time. I let it control and take over my life. I let it block my blessings, but God set me free. I had to choose *faith over fear.* I understand now that the enemy used fear as a gateway to destroy my life. He tried, but God's plans for my life will prevail. I do not regret putting my faith in God, and I will always put my faith in God.

Take a few minutes to reflect and write down these things:

1. Write down things that you put your faith in over God.
   Pray and repent for those things.

2. Write down all the things that you fear.
   Fear is not from God, so anything you fear must be broken off your life. Renounce and pray against the spirit of fear.

3. Write down things that God told you to do. Things that you did not do because of fear and unbelief in God.
   Pray, repent, and ask God for forgiveness. Forgive yourself as well.

4. Write down scriptures that God says about fear and lack of faith.
   Pray the scriptures over your life and replace the *fear with faith.*

Example: *"For God has not given us a spirit of fear, but of power and of love and of a sound mind." (II Timothy 1:7 NKJV)*
Prayer: Heavenly Father, your word says in *II Timothy 1:7* that you have not given me a spirit of fear, but of power, love, and a sound mind. I receive the power, love, and sound mind that you have given me. In the name of Jesus Christ,
Amen.

PRAYER

Dear Heavenly Father,

I repent for my sins and for the sins of my ancestors. I renounce and rebuke any demonic covenants and curses that were formed because of our lack of faith in you. We have not trusted you as we should have. We have put our trust and our faith in everything but you. I ask for your forgiveness and mercy upon my bloodline.

I repent for my lack of trust in you. I repent for allowing what I can see and feel in the physical change how I view you. Just because I cannot see you does not mean you do not exist. I pray you help me build my faith in you. Reveal to me any areas of my life where I am not fully trusting you. Help me walk by faith and not by sight.

Help me keep my faith in you no matter what my circumstances look like. I want what you want for my life. I trust the plans that you have for my life. Lord, redeem and restore any missed opportunities I lost due to not trusting you. I see the error in my ways and ask you to pour your mercy on my life.

Remove the spirit of fear out of my life. In *II Timothy 1:7*, your word says that *you have not given me a spirit of fear. You have given me power, love, and a sound mind.* I receive your power, love, and sound mind. I know that the spirit of fear is one reason I refused to trust and put faith in you. I repent for walking in fear. I know that fear is a weapon that Satan tries to use to destroy your people.

Whenever I fear, I am no longer aligned with you or your word. I declare that fear has no authority in my life any longer. I declare I will no longer allow fear and a lack of faith destroy your plans for my life. I come out of agreement with the spirit of fear. Lord, please remove all residue of fear from my life.

Cancel all demonic assignments on my life due to me breaking fear and disobedience off my life. I forgive myself for allowing fear and a lack of faith keep me out of alignment with you. I forgive myself for choosing to put my faith in things and the people of this world over you. From this day forward, I will put my faith in you no matter what it looks like. I am ready for this new season of *faith over fear.* Thank you for loving me and giving me grace even when I did not deserve it. Thank you for your mercy and protection. In the name of Jesus Christ, Amen.

3

HEALING

Healing is something that most people avoid. We avoid healing because we do not want to look at ourselves as broken, but at some point, we must get to the root of our pain. Until we get to the root of our pain, we will inflict our pain and trauma on those around us. Healing can be complicated, but it's necessary for our lives. God is a *healer*, so He wants us to seek Him for healing.

"He heals the brokenhearted and binds up their wounds."
(Psalms 147:3 NKJV)

When we are hurting, we view the world from a broken place. Some unhealed people view themselves as victims, so when someone says something to them, they are already in defense mode because they think they are being attacked. They are so guarded that they cannot even receive correction from a place of love. Others are so afraid of being hurt that they will try to hurt others before others can hurt them. They self-sabotage things and then wonder why their life is in shambles. They block their blessings because of ignorance and pride. They blame everyone else for their life going downhill. If they took the time to reflect, they would see that they are allowing unhealed trauma to destroy their lives.

Without healing, we will continue to have generational trauma and toxic relationships. We can heal, we can grow, and we can be better. The first step to healing is acknowledging that we need to heal. If we do not acknowledge it, how can we change it? God is close to those who are brokenhearted, and He wants to heal us from the inside out. God cannot heal us if we do not give Him our pain. We can give the pain we have to God and be set free, but we choose to carry the pain and allow it to spread through us like a virus. We let our pain cause us to hurt others, and we allow our pain to make us want to inflict pain on ourselves.

"The Lord is close to the brokenhearted; he rescues those whose spirits are crushed."
(Psalms 34:18 NLT)

Unhealed trauma can lead to so many demonic things, such as murder, abuse, adultery, drugs, alcohol, sexual sin, idolatry, suicide, toxic relationships, and all unhealthy addictions. None of those things are from God, and because we try to cover up our pain, we suffer for years. We attempt to portray a perfect image on the outside, but we are dying on the inside. *It's time to let that hurt go. It's time to give God the pain so that He can fully heal us. We do not have to carry the heavy burden of pain any longer! When we give it over to God, He will give us rest.*

"Then Jesus said, "Come to me, all of you who are weary and carry heavy burdens, and I will give you rest."
(Matthew 11:28 NLT)

When we are unhealed, we use our words as a weapon. Our words become venom. We use our words to hurt others because we are hurting. We fail to realize we are speaking word curses over ourselves and others. We should use our words to build up and not tear down. That is why it is so important to heal.

"Don't use foul or abusive language. Let everything you say be good and helpful, so that your words will be an encouragement to those who hear them."
(Ephesians 4:29 NLT)

Then, we seek things of this world for healing, leaving us more damaged. Drugs, alcohol, sex, and people cannot heal us. It is not anyone's job to heal us. It is our job to get healing for ourselves. Healing is something we must choose, and we must do the work to receive healing. We cannot continue to blame others for why we are still unhealed. Even if it is not our fault, it is still our responsibility to heal from our trauma. It is not always fair, and maybe we did not deserve many of the things that happened to us, but that is why we have to allow God to fight for us. He will fight for us, and He will redeem us. *God is the source we need for healing.*

When we heal, it comes with peace, love, joy, happiness, and forgiveness. We must heal if we want to have happy, healthy lives and relationships. If we are going to live a life that is pleasing to God, we must heal. We cannot keep living our lives in pain. We cannot keep passing down generational pain and trauma because of ignorance, unforgiveness, and pride. We talk about generational wealth, but what about generational healing? We do not have to let our children, grandchildren, or great-grandchildren suffer because we choose not to heal from our pain. *Our bloodline deserves to be set free, and it can be set free with God.*

It's time for us to change, heal, and grow. Let's break the strongholds that come with us, being unhealed from our lives for good. The pain and trauma was never ours. It was never meant for us to carry. It was something that Satan used to keep us in bondage. Let us choose the wholeness of God. We can be set free here and now. We have to give God the pain and let Him heal us. Not only will He heal us, but He can make it as if it never happened.

"The righteous cry out, and the Lord hears, And delivers them out of all their troubles."
(Psalms 34:17 NKJV)

MY TESTIMONY

My healing journey has had many ups and downs. I have cried many tears from painful experiences, but I have also had many tears of joy. I had to learn to see the beauty in my healing journey. I had to learn to trust God and let Him heal me instead of seeking healing in things of this world. I was broke, busted, and disgusted, but God...

Due to me being unhealed, I experienced some pain and trauma that I could have avoided if I had healed. Being unhealed led me to the wrong type of relationships and friendships. I surrounded myself with people who were not good for my life and held on to things that were not the best for me. I held on to toxic relationships because I allowed the trauma I experienced to block my ability to see people and things for what they were. I would overlook a lot of character flaws. I let the pain I experienced lead me away from God's will for my life.

I thought I could help people change, but they did not want to heal or grow. They inflicted their pain on me and others. Over time, I learned you cannot help someone who does not want to change because they will dislike you for it. Some people enjoy being victims because it gets them attention and sympathy. I did not want to be a victim. I wanted to be a victor. I did not want what happened to me to affect my life negatively. I wanted to be set free from my pain.

Having my heartbroken was a traumatic experience for me. During certain relationships, I allowed how I was being treated to make me feel worthless. I put my heart in the hands of people who did not fear or honor God. Anytime you put your heart in the hands of people, especially people who do not fear or honor God, your heart will be broken. I had also been living in sin. In the few relationships I had, I was in fornication. *Fornication is when you are having sex with someone you are not married to.* Anytime you are living in sin, you open up the door for demonic attacks on your life. The Bible makes it clear that sexual sin is wrong, but we do it anyway. I made that mistake, and I had to accept the consequences that came with sexual sin, including the pain I endured.

"Run from sexual sin! No other sin so clearly affects the body as this one does. For sexual immorality is a sin against your own body. Don't you realize that your body is the temple of the Holy Spirit, who lives in you and was given to you by God? You do not belong to yourself, for God bought you with a high price. So you must honor God with your body."
(1 Corinthians 6:18-20 NLT)

Over time, I surrendered and let God mend my broken heart. He put all the pieces back together. Not only did God put the pieces back together, but He also renewed my heart from the inside out. He gave me a new heart, and now I can live without the pain of my past holding me back. I will not make anyone suffer because of any past trauma I experienced. I can give people a clean slate, and the next romantic partner who comes into my life will have a healed, healthy version of me.

Now, I view life, love, and people differently. I do not have to self-sabotage anything out of fear. I do not have to inflict pain on others because I have been hurt. God has healed, changed, and made me whole in many areas of my life. I do not feel the same, and a lot of the pain I experienced feels as if it never happened. I can love people without fear, and *I can receive love*. Looking back on many things that occurred, I do not feel triggered. I feel God's peace, and I am thankful for His healing power.

Take a few minutes to reflect and write down these things:

1. Write down things that you need to heal from.
    Pray for God to reveal any hidden things you have not
    healed from. Give those things over to God.

2. Write down why you held on to those things for so long.
    You will have to forgive. Chapter 4 is about forgiveness. It will
    break down why forgiveness is so important.
    Pray and repent for not giving God your pain.

3. Write down scriptures that God says about healing.
    You have access to God's healing power.
    Pray the scriptures over your life.

PRAYER

Dear Heavenly Father,

I repent for my sins and for the sins of my ancestors when it comes to unhealed trauma. I renounce and rebuke any demonic covenants and curses that were formed because of pain and trauma. We have allowed the things we went through to destroy our family. We have allowed our pain to destroy relationships. We have allowed our pain to lead us into every type of sin.

We willingly and unwillingly hurt others because of our pain. We have passed down generational trauma because of pride and unforgiveness. I repent for not coming to you for healing, but for going to things of this world. I know that things of the world cannot heal me. I know you are the *source* for my healing.

I repent for hurting others, and I forgive those who have hurt me. I pray you help me heal in every area of my life. I no longer want to live in pain. I do not want to allow any pain and trauma to be passed down from generation to generation any longer. I ask for your forgiveness and grace upon my bloodline.

Reveal to me any areas of my life that I have not healed in. Help me keep my heart guarded so that I can avoid unnecessary pain. I know that when I am not aligned with you, I open the door for Satan to have authority in my life. I refuse to allow my pain to block any more of my blessings. Lord, redeem and restore everything I lost when I was unhealed.

Heal me from the inside out. Remove all residue of my trauma so that it feels as if it never happened. I receive the power of your healing in my life. I give all my trauma and pain to you. Your word says in *Matthew 11:28 to come to you with my heavy burdens, and you will give me rest.*

I am asking for your rest. I no longer want to suffer on the inside and try to hide it on the outside. I choose your peace and healing. I come out of agreement with any unhealed trauma. Let the blood of Jesus answer on my behalf against every attack of the enemy on my life. I declare I am not a victim. I declare I am a victor. I am whole, healthy, and healed. Thank you for your love, peace, and joy. In the name of Jesus Christ, Amen.

Healing

4

FORGIVENESS & REPENTANCE

Forgiveness is a thing that is usually hard to do, and sometimes it's hard to understand, especially when you are in a place where you have been hurt. It is even harder to forgive someone when you feel they have done something unforgivable. No matter what we think is unforgivable, God tells us to forgive. His word says in *Matthew 6:15 that if we do not forgive others, He will not forgive us.* Forgiveness is more for us than it is for the other person. We suffer when we are in unforgiveness.

"If you forgive those who sin against you, your heavenly Father will forgive you. But if you refuse to forgive others, your father will not forgive your sins."
(Matthew 6:14-15 NLT)

"And be kind to one another, tenderhearted, forgiving one another, even as God in Christ forgave you."
(Ephesians 4:32 NKJV)

One tactic of Satan is to have us in unforgiveness because he knows that as long as we are in unforgiveness, God will not forgive us. He also knows that we can never truly walk in our calling because our hearts will not be aligned with the word of God. So many people go to the grave in unforgiveness. They lived a life of bitterness and resentment because they would not forgive. They blocked many blessings from God because God will not bless our bitterness. Is that the type of life you want to live? I refuse to let unforgiveness steal anything that God has for me.

Unforgiveness opens up a door for the enemy to come into our lives. It hinders our prayers from being answered and blocks what God wants to do in our lives. It affects our heart, mind, body, and soul. It turns us into bitter people and ages us because it affects our health. We cannot afford to be in unforgiveness. It is also not worth the pain we endure due to carrying the burden of unforgiveness. *Forgiveness sets us free*, and we must allow God to fight for us. He will provide justice because He is a just God.

People may think that they are going up against you, but when you are living for God, they are not going up against you, they are going up against God. In the Bible, it talks about how someone who is your enemy is an enemy of God. *Your enemies will have no choice but to be at peace with you when your life pleases the Lord.* God does not play about His people, and we must remember that everyone is not a child of God. Some people have chosen who they serve. Pray for God to give them grace and mercy because they cannot win a battle against God.

"But if you are careful to obey him, following all my instructions, then I will be an enemy to your enemies, and I will oppose those who oppose you."
(Exodus 23:22 NLT)

"For the Lord your God is going with you! He will fight for you against your enemies, and he will give you victory!"
(Deuteronomy 20:4 NLT)

"The Lord himself will fight for you. Just stay calm."
(Exodus 14:14 NLT)

"When people's lives please the Lord, even their enemies are at peace with them."
(Proverbs 16:7 NLT)

Repentance

Feeling guilty is not repentance. Just because you cry and pray, it does not mean you have repented. Repentance is a heart posture, and it includes change. When you repent, you have to turn away from your sins. Many people say *"God knows my heart"* as an excuse for them to sin. Yes, God knows our hearts, which is even more of a reason for us to get our hearts right. He knows when our hearts are selfish, deceitful, and downright rotten. He also knows when our hearts are not aligned with His word.

We try to use God's grace as an excuse to justify our sins. God wants us to take accountability because unless we acknowledge our sins, we cannot change them. If we want to change, we cannot make excuses. It is time to stop making excuses and start making changes. We are not supposed to continue to commit the same sins. The Bible tells us, *"To go and sin no more."*

"She said, "No one, Lord." And Jesus said to her, "Neither do I condemn you; go and sin no more."
(John 8:11 NKJV)

We have to give God our hearts, repent, and grow. We have to learn from our mistakes and not repeat them, especially when we know better. If we repent and turn from our sins, they will be wiped clean. *We cannot expect anything to change in our lives if we do not change.* Before we pray and ask God to forgive us, we must forgive those who have trespassed against us.

"Now repent of your sins and turn to God, so that your sins may be wiped away."
(Acts 3:19 NLT)

The Bible says *if we humble ourselves, turn away from our sins, and seek God, He will hear from heaven, forgive us, and restore our land.* God allows us to repent and change. If we do not, we cannot be upset with the consequences that come into our lives. We cannot continue to waste time wallowing in our sins. We have to do the work, we have to change, we have to grow, and we have to live righteously. When God is telling us to let go of a person, place, thing, pride, unforgiveness, or any type of sin, we must let it go. If we continue to hold on to it, we are in disobedience. God wants us to let go of certain things because He sees what we cannot see. Even if we do not understand, we must obey what He tells us to do. *It's time for us to let it all go. It's time to pray, repent, and forgive those who have hurt us.* We must choose God's way.

> *"If my people who are called by My name will humble themselves, and pray and seek My face, and turn from their wicked ways, then I will hear from heaven, and will forgive their sin and heal their land."*
> *(II Chronicles 7:14 NKJV)*

MY TESTIMONY

I have had to repent for a lot of things. I had to forgive others and myself. I had to let go of the shame and guilt that came with living in sin. *God does not want us to live with shame or guilt.* It has been a learning process regarding forgiveness and repentance, but it has been worth it. Now, I try to repent daily because I genuinely want to change, and I want God to give me a clean slate every day. I do not want to be a prisoner of my past, nor do I want to hold anyone else as a prisoner of their past.

"But when you are praying, first forgive anyone you are holding a grudge against, so that your Father in heaven will forgive your sins, too."
(Mark 11:25 NLT)

Thinking about forgiveness lets me know how much I have grown on my walk with God. I get to reflect on my journey of forgiveness. It has not been easy, especially when you have to forgive someone who repeats the same offense. It is also difficult to forgive when the person is not remorseful. I have learned to forgive, anyway. I try to forgive *quickly* when an offense happens because I do not want to carry any unforgiveness in my heart, and I do not want to become bitter. I never want to deal with the demonic strongholds that come with unforgiveness.

"Then Peter came to him and asked, "Lord, how often should I forgive someone who sins against me? Seven times?" "No, not seven times," Jesus replied, "but seventy times seven!"
(Matthew 18:21-22 NLT)

No matter what they have done, there is no person I have not forgiven. It feels amazing to have a clean heart. *I cannot afford to be in unforgiveness because it costs too much.* I let it steal years of my life, and I refuse to let it take any more time from me. None of us can afford to carry unforgiveness in our hearts. The sooner we realize it, the sooner we can heal.

I learned a lot from my divorce. One of the main things I learned was how to forgive. I had a very messy divorce. It was so toxic it took many years for things to improve. It was one of the most toxic things I have had to experience. It felt like a movie because it did not feel like my life. Honestly, I was not prepared for all the spiritual attacks that came with my divorce. I had to deal with lies being told about me, things being posted about me online, harassment, being disrespected, and even threats being made. It was heavy *spiritual warfare*.

God revealed to me that what I was up against was very *demonic*. I am thankful He showed me that what I was experiencing was *spiritual* because I would have let my heart for people blind me. I did not understand why all of those things were happening to me, but later, I learned anytime you are living in sin, you give the demonic kingdom authority in your life. Also, when you are in a relationship with someone, and they are living in sin, they open up the door for Satan to run rampant in your home and your life. *You could lose your life being attached to the wrong people.* That is why it's imperative to be aligned with the word of God.

After leaving my marriage, I thought I would be at peace. In that season, I wanted to be happy and whole. I also wanted to give my children a better life. I did not want them to grow up in a toxic environment. Having to deal with all those spiritual attacks took a toll on me mentally, emotionally, physically, and spiritually. God wanted me to forgive, so I had to forgive. I had to forgive a person who showed no remorse and repeatedly tried to hurt me. It was challenging and felt unfair, but I knew God would work everything out for my good.

I had to learn how to fight properly against spiritual warfare. I had to learn how to fight in prayer. I took matters into my own hands in the past, but I knew this was different. It was a higher level of spiritual warfare. Not only did I have to deal with all that unnecessary drama, but I also lost many people in that season. It was hurtful... I did not know it then, but God was closing doors that needed to be shut. I am genuinely thankful for the people who supported me during that time.

With God, I was able to overcome it all. Sometimes, when I would pray, I would ask God to bring the truth to light. Not my truth, not my ex-husband's truth, but the truth. I knew eventually the truth would come to light. I knew that the lies being spoken about me would be proven to be untrue. God had already been working on me and was using me as a *light*. No matter how much dirt was being thrown on my name, my light would shine regardless. *When you truly live for God, it cannot be hidden*, so people will eventually see the light of God in you.

I did not allow the pain I felt to interfere with who God was calling me to be. I did not post hateful things in retaliation. I dealt with it all privately. *I went to war in prayer, and I let God fight for me.* I knew that the goal of the enemy was to make my heart bitter and have me in unforgiveness so that I would not be aligned with God. His ultimate goal was to take my life. Satan was threatened by what God wanted to do in my life. He tried to destroy me from the inside out, but God…*He is faithful.*

Sometimes, I would fall into the traps of the enemy. I would get emotional and argue back when I felt disrespected. After, I would realize it was a trap. Eventually, I got to a point where it did not bother me anymore. Occasionally, over the years, I would pray for my ex-husband, and I would tell our daughters to pray for him. I would pray for God to give him grace and mercy. I would also pray for God to heal him, change his heart, and to spare his life. I would pray for God to spare his life because I know that the *wages of sin is death*. People would tell me they could not deal with what I had to deal with. I knew I would not be able to deal with it either without God. *God fought for me, built my character, and changed my heart.*

I do not hate my ex-husband, and honestly, I never did. I still pray for him, and I wish him the best. I always wanted the best for him, and I still do. Sometimes, when we go through things and are upset with someone, we want bad things to happen to them. That way of thinking is wrong. That is why we have to forgive and heal. Some people thought they knew my heart, but the heart I had during that time was a heart of *love* because God wanted me to walk in love. I had a heart of *grace* and a heart of *peace*. I no longer wanted revenge or to make anyone feel the pain that they had caused me.

Finally, in March 2023, almost seven years after our divorce, my ex-husband apologized to me via email. Even though the disrespect was public, he apologized privately. It took a long time, but I knew God was working. I had already forgiven him and had some closure, so I did not expect an apology. I feel like God wanted me to receive that apology. I emailed him back to apologize for the things that I had done. I apologized before, but he was so upset that he could not receive my apology. I was not a perfect wife, but I tried my best to be. I tried my best, but it was not good enough. *I learned that no matter how good of a person you are, you will never be good enough for the wrong person.* You will never be good enough for the wrong person because they will not appreciate you. Don't let it change how you feel about yourself.

I feel so blessed because my heart is free despite everything I went through. I gave everything to God, and now I do not have to fight any battles alone. I know how important forgiveness is and that I can forgive with God. I know *repentance is vital,* and *we are not our mistakes.* As long as we have air in our lungs, we can change. *Never let what you have been through lead you away from God or change your heart. Repent quickly and forgive even quicker. Kill unforgiveness at the root because if you do not, it will destroy you from the inside out.*

Take a few minutes to reflect and write down these things:

1. Write down people you need to forgive.
   <u>Pray and forgive them.</u>

2. Write down things you need to repent for.
   <u>Repent and ask God to forgive you.</u>

3. Write down things that you need to forgive yourself for.
   <u>Pray and forgive yourself.</u>

4. Write down scriptures about forgiveness and repentance.
   <u>Pray the scriptures over your life.</u>
   <u>*Receive God's forgiveness.*</u>

PRAYER

Dear Heavenly Father,

I repent for my sins and for the sins of my ancestors. I renounce and rebuke any demonic covenants and curses formed because of our lack of unforgiveness and repentance. We have held on to unforgiveness and bitterness. We have tried to take matters into our own hands. We have repaid vengeance for vengeance. We have been full of anger and pride.

I repent for sinning against you. I repent for allowing Satan's voice to be louder than your voice. I repent for putting my emotions above your word. I pray you show me how to fight correctly. When I am wrong, correct me. Help me be a light even when I am experiencing spiritual warfare.

I pray you block every demonic spirit trying to attack me. Help me seek you daily and die to my flesh. Cleanse all the toxic thinking I have when it comes to forgiveness. Help me always forgive others. I come out of agreement with the spirit of unforgiveness. Redeem and restore all the years I lost, being bitter, angry, and prideful. Cancel every demonic assignment on my life.

Let the blood of Jesus Christ answer on my behalf. Re-establish my life to your divine appointed timeline. Lord, I forgive all the people who have hurt me. I forgive myself for all the things I have done. I am ready to accept your will for my life.

I am prepared to change, and I want to change. I receive your forgiveness, mercy, and grace. Thank you for loving me and protecting me. Thank you for fighting on my behalf. Thank you for the opportunity to repent and turn away from my sins. Thank you for your forgiveness. In the name of Jesus Christ, Amen.

If you have anything to repent for, make sure to include your prayer in this prayer.

5

WISDOM & DISCERNMENT

Most people are wise in their own eyes but lack godly wisdom. The Bible says that *we should not be wise in our own eyes or impressed by our wisdom.* We seek worldly knowledge, and we are proud of our worldly titles and achievements, but those things mean nothing without God. *What good is it for us to gain the world but lose our soul?* Are those things worth more than our relationship with God? In my opinion, *nothing is more important than our relationship with God.*

> *"Do not be wise in your own eyes; Fear the Lord and depart from evil."*
> *(Proverbs 3:7 NKJV)*

> *"And what do you benefit if you gain the whole world but lose your own soul?"*
> *(Mark 8:36 NLT)*

God wants us to seek Him for wisdom. We should seek Him as our primary source of knowledge. We should pray for wisdom, knowledge, and understanding in every area of our lives. We have access to knowledge, but we choose to be ignorant. Our ignorance is not an excuse to sin against God or to avoid the consequences of

53

our actions.

"Wisdom is the principal thing; Therefore, get wisdom. And in all your getting, get understanding."
(Proverbs 4:7 NKJV)

Wisdom is one of the most powerful things that we can have. We should seek wisdom from God daily. If we can seek worldly knowledge, we can seek godly wisdom. The Bible says that *God's people are destroyed for lack of knowledge;* it does not say the people who live for Satan; it says, *"My people are destroyed for lack of knowledge."* If we do not get godly wisdom, we will be destroyed.

"For wisdom is better than rubies, and all the things one may desire cannot be compared with her."
(Proverbs 8:11 NKJV)

"My people are destroyed for lack of knowledge. Because you have rejected knowledge, I also will reject you from being priest for Me; Because you have forgotten the law of your God, I also will forget your children."
(Hosea 4:6 NKJV)

God tells us that if we lack wisdom, ask Him, and He will give it without reproach. *We can have all the knowledge in the world, and it still will not replace the need for God in our lives.* The Bible gives us the tools we need to live a life that is pleasing to the Lord. A great source to seek wisdom is by reading *Proverbs.* Proverbs is full of wisdom, guidance, and discernment. It gives us tools that can *save our lives* from destruction. There is no point in getting wisdom if we are not going to apply it.

"If any of you lacks wisdom, let him ask of God, who gives to all liberally and without reproach, and it will be given to him."
(James 1:5 NKJV)

When we know better, we should do better. The issue is when people know better but still choose to make choices that are not wise. As we gain wisdom, we should help others along the way. In this season, *it is time to live a life full of wisdom. We cannot continue to be ignorant when we have full access to the knowledge of God.*

Discernment

Right now, we are in a time where most people lack discernment. We call wrong, right, and right wrong. We are easily deceived and manipulated. We lack basic discernment and spiritual discernment. We do not know if we are going or coming. We let our heart for people block our ability to recognize when someone is a counterfeit. When God reveals who someone is, we do not believe it. When we finally realize we were deceived, it is usually too late. God tries to warn us about people, but we ignore Him. We get so focused on the desires of our hearts that we overlook what God is trying to show us. *We cannot afford to lack discernment in any area of our lives.*

If we lack discernment, we need to ask God to give us the ability to discern. We need to discern what God wants us to do, where God wants us to go, and with whom God wants us to surround ourselves. We should be tired of being deceived by people who claim to serve God but are wolves in sheep's clothing. We should also be tired of being deceived by people who want to have romantic relationships with us and by people who claim to be our friends. Deception is at an all-time high, and we continue to fall into the trap. We fall into the trap because our hearts are not aligned with God's word.

"Beware of false prophets, who come to you in sheep's clothing, but inwardly they are ravenous wolves."
(Matthew 7:15 NKJV)

We have to stop putting people on a pedestal and idolizing people; it is idolatry, and God hates idolatry. *Idolatry is anything we put above and love more than our obedience to God.* It can be a relationship, your kids, money, sex, etc. It also includes worshiping other artificial things and calling them God. When we idolize people, they can do no wrong in our eyes unless they have done something wrong to us. Even when they have done us wrong, we make excuses for them to satisfy our desires. We enable these people to deceive, manipulate, and inflict harm on us and others.

We have to get to a place where we are not impressed by the titles and achievements of man. *What does their fruit show us?* Satan uses deception and manipulation to bring the wrong people into our lives.

55

We overlook the red flags and repeatedly fall for who people pretend to be. Some people we think are living for God are wolves in sheep's clothing. They are *counterfeits* that look and sound like the real thing, but they are not the real thing. We judge them based on their appearance and fake theatrics, but *God looks at the heart*, and their hearts are far from Him. That is why we need spiritual discernment. We need to take heed of what God is revealing to us. *It's time to receive and apply God's wisdom and discernment to our lives.*

"But the Lord said to Samuel, "Do not look at his appearance or at his physical stature, because I have refused him. For the Lord does not see as man sees; for man looks at the outward appearance, but the Lord looks at the heart."
(I Samuel 16:7 NKJV)

"If you are wise and understand God's ways, prove it by living an honorable life, doing good works with the humility that comes from wisdom."
(James 3:13 NLT)

"So be careful how you live. Don't live like fools, but like those who are wise."
(Ephesians 5:15 NLT)

"For the Lord gives wisdom; From His mouth come knowledge and understanding; He stores up sound wisdom for the upright; He is a shield to those who walk uprightly; He guards the paths of justice, And preserves the way of His saints."
(Proverbs 2:6-8 NKJV)

"When wisdom enters your heart, And knowledge is pleasant to your soul, Discretion will preserve you; Understanding will keep you,"
(Proverbs 2:10-11 NKJV)

MY TESTIMONY

Having wisdom and discernment is very important in my life. I have been wise in my own eyes, such as feeling as if I knew more than I did. Once I gave my life to Christ, I humbled myself and sought godly wisdom over worldly knowledge. I always pray and ask God to give me wisdom in every area of my life. I refuse to be ignorant when it comes to the knowledge of God. I try to seek wisdom daily.

I have made many decisions without seeking God first. It was not wise, and it came with negative consequences. That is why it is always best to *pray and wait for God to lead you before making decisions*. When we make decisions without God, we end up out of His will. Then, we suffer the consequences of our choices, which feel horrible. You will know when something is from God because you will feel His peace. Sometimes, explaining His peace is hard, but it feels quiet, relaxed, and sure. It comes without confusion. Anytime you feel confused about anything, it is not from God; *God is not the author of confusion*. Satan brings confusion into our lives to deceive us. Never make a decision when you are confused. You will most likely end up making the wrong choice.

I have made a fair share of decisions while I was confused. The week I got married, there was a lot of confusion, frustration, and doubt. At the time, I did not realize how important those feelings were or that they were warnings from God. I remember the day I got married; I felt uneasy, and I did not have peace. Everyone around me had already prepared for that day, making me feel like I had to go through with it. I wanted to marry my ex-husband, but I had doubts about him not being ready for marriage. Even though I had my doubts, I went through with it, anyway. I let my love for him block my discernment. Years later, when I was in the process of my divorce, God showed me I did not have peace the day I got married.

It was a huge revelation. God revealed to me all the red flags I overlooked while dating. I was able to go back and see the red flags I had ignored. A lot of them were *deal breakers*. I had lowered my standards and went against some of my morals and values. *We should never lower our standards or go against our morals and values, especially when those things align with God's word.* I do not regret the relationship because my daughters came from that relationship, but I wish I had married someone who truly loved me. Someone that God had for my life. I take it all in as a lesson. I know what Satan meant for evil; God will use it for my good. *I believe God will restore and redeem everything I lost.*

"You intended to harm me, but God intended it all for good. He brought me to this position so I could save the lives of many people."
(Genesis 50:20 NLT)

Spiritual discernment is another thing I lacked. I let the heart I have for people blind my discernment of who they truly were. I have been deceived so many times in every area of my life. I have learned from it. Now, I try to discern and *test every spirit.* I cannot afford to be aligned with the wrong people or things. I let God show me who people are, and I try to never doubt it because He is never wrong. I trust God even when I do not understand. Whenever I have a bad feeling about something or someone later on, I realize that what I felt was correct. I have had people try to use my past trauma to make me believe that what I felt strongly about was wrong. It was not wrong; it was spot on. Whenever you have a bad feeling about someone, trust it. You should always pray about it, but trust what you feel at that moment. *That warning could save your life.*

There have been times when I thought certain people liked me, but I would sense a jealous spirit in them. I would overlook my feelings because I wanted to see the good in people. Those people would smile in my face, but deep down, they were jealous of me. I was confused when I could sense the jealousy because I felt like I had nothing for them to be jealous of, but people will be jealous of you for anything. Sometimes, people can see the anointing from God on your life even if you do not see it. You never want to stay around jealous people because they will plot on you and try to sabotage you. You will think they are trying to help you, but they will try to keep you from prospering in life.

Jealousy has the potential to escalate to murder. That is why we must be careful who we allow into our lives. *Iron sharpens iron,* but

58

many people will try to break you instead of sharpening you. We will attract all kinds of people into our lives, but we have control over who we *allow* in our lives. We do not have to accept everything offered to us. *We do not have to settle, and we should test every spirit.* Eventually, the true nature of a person will be revealed. People can only pretend for so long. I do not take any of my experiences lightly. I want to help others avoid the lessons I have had to learn the hard way. I will continue to seek godly wisdom and spiritual discernment in every area of my life.

"You want what you don't have, so you scheme and kill to get it. You are jealous of what others have, but you can't get it, so you fight and wage war to take it away from them. Yet you don't have what you want because you don't ask God for it. And even when you ask, you don't get it because your motives are all wrong—you want only what will give you pleasure."
(James 4:2-3 NLT)

"For jealousy and selfishness are not God's kind of wisdom. Such things are earthly, unspiritual, and demonic. For wherever there is jealousy and selfish ambition, there you will find disorder and evil of every kind."
(James 3:15-16 NLT)

"But the wisdom that is from above is first pure, then peaceable, gentle, willing to yield, full of mercy and good fruits, without partiality and without hypocrisy."
(James 3:17 NKJV)

"He who walks with wise men will be wise, But the companion of fools will be destroyed."
(Proverbs 13:20 NKJV)

"Guard your heart above all else, for it determines the course of your life."
(Proverbs 4:23 NLT)

Take a few minutes to reflect and write down these things:

1. Write down areas in your life where you lack wisdom.
   Pray for God to give you wisdom in those areas.

2. Write down areas of your life where you need discernment.
   Pray for God to give you discernment and the ability to
   discern spirits.

3. Write down things that you need to forgive yourself for.
   Pray and forgive yourself.

4. Write down scriptures about wisdom and discernment.
   Pray the scriptures over your life.

PRAYER

Dear Heavenly Father,

I repent for my sins and for the sins of my ancestors when it comes to wisdom and discernment. I renounce and rebuke any demonic covenants and curses formed because of a lack of wisdom and discernment. We have allowed our ignorance to lead us away from you. We have allowed our ignorance to be passed down from generation to generation. I ask for your forgiveness and grace upon my bloodline.

I repent for not seeking wisdom and discernment from you. I repent for choosing ignorance over knowledge. I repent for denying your wisdom. I repent for being naïve and not discerning spirits. I repent for ignoring your warnings about people. Help me no longer allow the heart I have for people block what you reveal to me about them. When you show me who someone is, I will believe it.

I have idolized people and things. I repent for idolizing people and things of this world. I will seek your word as my source of knowledge. I repent for choosing the wrong things when I knew what was right. I repent for coming into agreement with things that are against your word.

Lord, redeem and restore everything I lost while living a life of rebellion and pride. I no longer want to entertain foolishness. I come out of agreement with ignorance. I want to live a life full of wisdom. Give me the ability to quickly discern what is not right for my life.

Thank you for your wisdom and discernment. Thank you for your forgiveness. Thank you for your guidance. I receive your wisdom and discernment. I declare I am wise. I will apply your wisdom and discernment to my life. Thank you for all you do in my life. In the name of Jesus Christ, Amen.

6

ACCOUNTABILITY & CORRECTION

R ight now, we are in a time where people do not want to be held accountable for their actions. They want to do whatever they please without being corrected. Everything is considered judgment, and God's grace is being used as an excuse to sin. People say, *"I'm covered by God's grace. Who are you to judge me?"* God sends people to warn and correct us when we do things unaligned with His word. When He sends them to warn us, we need to take heed. If we do not, we are in disobedience.

"If you reject discipline, you only harm yourself; but if you listen to correction, you grow in understanding."
(Proverbs 15:32 NLT)

"He who disdains instruction despises his own soul, But he who heeds rebuke gets understanding."
(Proverbs 15:32 NKJV)

We instantly put up a guard and feel as though we're being attacked. It's important to remember that not everyone is attacking us; *some people correct us from a place of love.* Instead of receiving the correction, we choose to be prideful. We should always pray when we receive a word from someone, but that is no excuse to ignore the word, especially when we know we are doing wrong. Despite knowing we're not aligned with God's word, we become prideful and refuse to listen. We choose to argue with people. Our pride is irrelevant; we will fall if we remain in pride. We should strive for self-accountability and embrace being held accountable by others. Often, we hear people talk about grace, how no one can judge them, and how nobody is perfect. Although nobody is perfect, we cannot use that as an excuse for our behavior.

"Pride goes before destruction, And a haughty spirit before a fall."
(Proverbs 16:18 NKJV)

When God sends someone to warn us, they are usually sent to save us before destruction. If that person is truly sent by God, disrespecting them is disrespectful to God. The Bible says, *"Be quick to listen, slow to speak, and slow to anger."* So, when God sends someone to correct us, we need to be quick to listen, slow to anger, and slow to speak. We have to be able to receive correction and accountability, especially when it is from God. God corrects those He loves, and He disciplines those He loves. Just as He corrects, loves, and gives us grace, He also punishes us.

"Understand this, my dear brothers and sisters: You must all be quick to listen, slow to speak, and slow to get angry."
(James 1:19 NLT)

"For whom the Lord loves He corrects, Just as a father the son in whom he delights."
(Proverbs 3:12 NKJV)

"For the Lord disciplines those he loves, and he punishes each one he accepts as his child."
(Hebrews 12:6 NLT)

Before God sends someone to warn us, He has already warned us, and we ignored the warning. Our reaction is to argue and become upset with the person who is sent to correct us and hold us accountable. Our lives are on the line. It's time to repent, turn from our sins, and not go back because God has sent us warning after warning, and we continue to disobey Him. When we disobey God, there are always consequences, and we do not get to choose the consequences. To avoid facing negative consequences, we must take heed of God's instructions.

While we often discuss God's grace, love, and mercy, we tend to neglect His correction and accountability. He is a just God, so we should not think we can continue abusing His grace, and then saying, *"Nobody can judge me."* The Bible says to judge righteously. We should read the Bible more and stop trying to seek things to fit our lukewarm lifestyle.

God does not run off our emotions. Everything is not about how we feel and what we want. We cannot continue to play around when it comes to our salvation. *John 7:24* says *for us not to judge according to appearance, but to judge with righteous judgment.* We judge based on appearance regarding how someone looks, but we do not believe in judgment when it comes to accountability. *We are supposed to judge righteously,* and we should because deception is at an all-time high. We are also supposed to look at the fruit of a person. *We will know them by their fruit,* so if we have to judge off of someone's fruit, we have to judge them, and that is biblical.

"Do not judge according to appearance, but judge with righteous judgment."
(John 7:24 NKJV)

"You can identify them by their fruit, that is, by the way they act. Can you pick grapes from thornbushes, or figs from thistles? A good tree produces good fruit, and a bad tree produces bad fruit. A good tree can't produce bad fruit, and a bad tree can't produce good fruit. So every tree that does not produce good fruit is chopped down and thrown into the fire. Yes, just as you can identify a tree buy its fruit, so you can identify people by their actions."
(Matthew 7:16-20 NLT)

MY TESTIMONY

As a kid, I would cry if someone corrected me. They did not even have to yell. I was very sensitive, and my feelings were easily hurt. I did not like being yelled at and I did not need to be yelled at because the correction was enough. I did not want to learn things the hard way. A lot of the things I learned were from other people's mistakes and bad choices. I did not want the consequences they received, so I would try to avoid the same mistakes.

As I got older, I would be in defense mode when people corrected me because I was so used to having to have my guard up. I would feel like I was being attacked, so sometimes I rejected accountability from others. Over time, I embraced accountability and correction because I wanted to be better. I also knew when I was in the wrong, so I would hold myself accountable and own up to the things I did.

The more I grew in Christ, the more I realize the importance of accountability and correction. As parents, we have to correct our children, and in the moment, correction never feels good. When you love someone, you correct them because you want them to know right from wrong. You also want them to know that there are consequences for bad behavior. That is how God is with us. He wants us to be at our best, so He corrects us when we are wrong.

When I had to deal with certain consequences for my actions, I would be upset, but I had to take accountability for my choices and the sins that I committed. I allowed the desires of my flesh to lead me away from God. I had to take full responsibility, repent, and change. I had to understand that I did not get to choose the consequences of my actions. Being in a situation where my life was on the line showed me a lot. I got to understand the meaning of the wages of sin being death. Disobedience almost cost me my life. *None of the worldly pleasures matter when the goal of the enemy is to take your life.*

I honestly believe *nothing in this world should be more important than our relationship with God,* and I do not think that *there is anything worth sinning against God for.* If we have to sin to get something, we most likely will have to sin to keep it. If it is not from God, I do not want it. I try to avoid willingly living in sin because it is not worth my salvation. I want God's accountability and correction in my life because I want to be better. The more I grow in my walk with Christ, the more I love obeying God's word. Ultimately, I want to hear, *"Well done, my good and faithful servant."*

Take a few minutes to reflect and write down these things:

1. Write down areas in your life where you lack discipline.
   <u>Pray for God to give you discipline in those areas.</u>

2. Write down areas in your life where you need accountability.
   <u>Pray for God to help you be accountable and to send people to help hold you accountable.</u>

3. Write down excuses you make for your poor choices.
   <u>Pray and repent for your lack of accountability.</u>

4. Write down scriptures that talk about accountability and correction.
   <u>Pray the scriptures over your life.</u>

PRAYER

Dear Heavenly Father,

I repent for my sins and for the sins of my ancestors when it comes to accountability and correction. I renounce and rebuke any demonic covenants and curses formed because of our lack of accountability and correction. We have allowed our pride to lead us away from you. We have taken your grace for granted. We have denied your correction and rejected the correction you sent others to give us. I ask for your forgiveness and mercy upon my bloodline.

I repent for ignoring your warnings. I repent for being prideful and for not being open to correction. I repent for not being slow to speak, slow to listen, or slow to anger. I repent for getting upset when it comes to correction and accountability. Help me stop allowing the pain I have experienced in the past to block my ability to receive correction. When you show me what I am doing wrong, I will listen.

I repent for coming into agreement with things that are against your word. I come out of agreement with the spirit of rebellion and disobedience. I know you correct those you love, so I come into agreement with your accountability and correction. Lord, redeem and restore everything I lost because I ignored your warnings. Help me give correction from a place of love. When I get off track, help me quickly get back on track.

I repent for doing wrong when I knew what was right. I no longer want to choose pride over you. I no longer want to let my feelings get the best of me. Give me the ability to quickly follow your word.

Thank you for your accountability and correction. Thank you for sending people to warn me and to save my life from destruction. Thank you for your forgiveness. Thank you for your guidance. I receive your correction. I declare I will apply your word to my life. Thank you for all you do in my life. In the name of Jesus Christ, Amen.

7

YOUR PRIVATE LIFE

Many of us are not aligned with God regarding our private lives. *We speak His name with our mouths, but our hearts are far from Him.* Most people want a platform, so they use God's name to build one. They will speak God's name publicly but privately live their life serving Satan. People do not think they serve him, but they do by willingly living in sin. They want public praise more than they want to serve God. They want God's blessings but do not want to live according to His word. The Bible tells us *to come out from among them.* So, we are not supposed to be living like the world. Yet, we choose to follow the ways of the world above God.

"Therefore "Come out from among them And be separate, says the Lord. Do not touch what is unclean, And I will receive you."
(II Corinthians 6:17 NKJV)

"They will act religious, but they will reject the power that could make them godly. Stay away from people like that!"
(2 Timothy 3:5 NLT)

"But know this, that in the last days perilous times will come: For men will be lovers of themselves, lovers of money, boasters, proud, blasphemers, disobedient

to parents, unthankful, unholy, unloving, unforgiving, slanderers, without self-control, brutal, despisers of good, traitors, headstrong, haughty, lovers of pleasure rather than lovers of God, having a form of godliness but denying its power. And from such people turn away!"
(II Timothy 3:1-5) NKJV)

The Bible also says *we will know them by their fruit.* People who have *discernment* can see when we lack spiritual fruit. They can see when our walk with God is not authentic. *How can we expect to lead others to Christ if we are not connected to Him?* We make excuses for our willing sin, but God is not a God of excuses, nor does He want people to use His name in vain. A time is coming when those who have been claiming God's name publicly but privately serving Satan will be exposed. God will eventually remove His grace and mercy from those who play with His name.

"You will know them by their fruits. Do men gather grapes from thornbushes or figs from thistles? Even so, every good tree bears good fruit, but a bad tree bears bad fruit. A good tree cannot bear bad fruit, nor can a bad tree bear good fruit. Every tree that does not bear good fruit is cut down and thrown into the fire."
(Matthew 7:16-19 NKJV)

Serving God needs to be in spirit and in truth. The *wages of sin is death.* We might not die at the moment, but things will die, whether it is a relationship, your heart, or your relationship with God. One of the easiest sins to fall into is sexual sin because it's so accessible. The media promotes porn, masturbation, threesomes, adultery, and fornication. Promiscuity is at an all-time high. As believers, It's important to *protect our hearts and practice self-control. If we submit to God and resist the Devil, he will flee from us. We must die to ourselves daily, take up our cross, and follow Christ.* We cannot continue to live like the world. Why do we, as believers, try to emulate a world that hates God and serves Satan?

"For the wages of sin is death, but the gift of God is eternal life in Christ Jesus our Lord."
(Romans 6:23 NKJV)

"Therefore submit to God. Resist the devil and he will flee from you."

(James 4:7 NKJV)

"If the Good News we preach is hidden behind a veil, it is hidden only from people who are perishing. Satan, who is the god of this world, has blinded the minds of those who don't believe. They are unable to see the glorious light of the Good News. They don't understand this message about the glory of Christ, who is the exact likeness of God."
(2 Corinthians 4:3-4 NLT)

Jesus came to bring a sword, not a pamper, and a baby bottle to satisfy our fleshly desires. A sword cuts, and it comes to bring change. It will turn people against us, but we must choose who we will serve. Will we serve God, the Creator of all, or Satan, the god of this world? We have to get right, or we will get left behind. Being lukewarm has to end immediately because God will spit us out of His mouth. *We cannot serve God and this world.* We must choose one or the other because we cannot have both. Either we are in or out. We must be hot or cold because we cannot be in the middle.

"Do not think that I came to bring peace on earth. I did not come to bring peace but a sword."
(Matthew 10:34 NKJV)

"I know your works, that you are neither cold nor hot. I could wish you were cold or hot. So then, because you are lukewarm, and neither cold nor hot, I will vomit you out of My mouth."
(Revelation 3:15-16 NKJV)

"No one can serve two masters. For you will hate one and love the other; you will be devoted to one and despise the other. You cannot serve God and be enslaved to money."
(Matthew 6:24 NLT)

God sees everything and knows when we lead others astray by how we live our lives privately. He knows when we are leading people into sin. Anytime we are in fornication with someone, we are leading them away from God. *How can we say we love someone, yet lead them away from God to please our flesh?* No matter what the excuse is, we cannot claim to love God but privately continue to sin against Him. God will not be mocked, and those living double lives will eventually be exposed.

"Nothing in all creation is hidden from God. Everything is naked and exposed before his eyes, and he is the one to whom we are accountable."
(Hebrews 4:13 NLT)

"Do not be deceived, God is not mocked; for whatever a man sows, that he will also reap."
(Galatians 6:7 NKJV)

People think because they pray for people, minister to them, and say God's name, that He is pleased with them, but if they are willingly living in sin, God is not pleased. We cannot claim to repent and not change our behavior. That is not repentance. We cannot claim to serve God but live for Satan. *When we truly live for God, the fruit will be evident.* It does not matter who we pretend to be publicly; eventually, the things we do in private will come to light. Demons know demons, and demons also know when someone is righteous.

The righteous know when someone is pretending to be righteous, especially when using spiritual discernment. It is not about perfection. It is about genuinely aligning with God. We have to choose to serve and live for God publicly and privately. We have to stop getting comfortable living in sin. We cannot continue to use God's grace as an excuse to willingly sin. *Grace was never meant for us to take for granted.* It is intended to cover our mistakes. Yes, God blesses, forgives, and loves us, but He is also a jealous God, and He will never be okay with us claiming to serve Him but living like everyone else in the world.

"Their loyalty is divided between God and the world, and they are unstable in everything they do."
(James 1:8 NLT)

Do You Know of God, or Do You Know God?

Many people know of God but do not truly know Him because when you know God, *you revere Him, and your life will be a reflection of Him publicly and privately.* When you know of Him, you take His grace for granted, but when you know Him, you understand that living for

Him will be uncomfortable. When you know of Him, you say His name publicly, but privately, you worship and serve Satan. When you know of Him, you get upset about accountability and correction. When you know Him, you know that accountability and correction is vital. You also know that we must judge righteously, and that God corrects those He loves. When you know of Him, you speak His name for public praise, financial gain, and other benefits that come with the name of God. When you know Him, you speak His name to give Him the glory, and you do not care about public praise because you want to hear, *"Well done, my good and faithful servant."* When you know of Him, you want to be a part of the crowd, so you choose to be lukewarm and water down His word. You care more about the world's approval than God's approval. When you know Him, you understand it is a broad and narrow road. You choose to walk that narrow road even if you have to do it alone. When you know God, there is no way that you cannot be transformed into a new person. *God is too powerful for you to be in His presence and not be changed.*

"Everything is pure to those whose hearts are pure. But nothing is pure to those who are corrupt and unbelieving, because their minds and consciences are corrupted. Such people claim they know God, but they deny him by the way they live. They are detestable and disobedient, worthless for doing anything good."
(Titus 1: 15-16 NLT)

"But the gateway to life is very narrow and the road is difficult, and only a few ever find it."
(Matthew 7:14 NLT)

God revealed to me that you can be in church for many years and still not know Him. You might think you know God, but you do not know Him. Unforgiveness, excuses, pride, and ignorance hinder your ability to truly know God. Your excuses do not change His word, your worship and praise mean nothing if your heart is not aligned with God, and your ministry built on pride and greed is not pleasing to God. Having people worship you as if you are God is not aligned with God. God did not call people to steal from His flock, He did not call people to lie to His flock, and He did not call people to abuse His flock. *He called people to lead His flock to Him and only Him.*

75

Anytime you say God's name, you should know it comes with power, obedience, sacrifice, wisdom, change, dying to yourself daily, favor, godly authority, a humble spirit, a heart to serve, a loving heart, a forgiving heart, faith, anointing, trusting God, fruits of the spirit, and the Holy Spirit. Living for God is not always convenient, nor is it always easy. Many are called, but few are chosen because it's human nature to be selfish and to want to choose the flesh over the spirit.

"For many are called, but few are chosen."
(Matthew 22:14 NKJV)

As I wrote this, God led every word. It is not me; it is all Him, and I thank God for using me as a vessel. If you know your heart is not truly aligned with God, ask Him to help you get it right, because we cannot afford to waste time. *We must be transformed by allowing God to renew our minds.* Although this message may be difficult to hear, it is not my message, it is God's message. This message may bring conviction, and that is exactly what it is supposed to bring. This message may step on your toes, but it stepped on my toes first.

"And do not be conformed to this world, but be transformed by the renewing of your mind, that you may prove what is that good and acceptable and perfect will of God."
(Romans 12:2 NKJV)

"This is the message we heard from Jesus and now declare to you: God is light, and there is no darkness in him at all. So we are lying if we say we have fellowship with God but go on living in spiritual darkness; we are not practicing the truth. But if we are living in the light, as God is in the light, then we have fellowship with each other, and the blood of Jesus, his Son, cleanses us from all sin."
(1 John 1:5-7 NLT)

"And the judgment is based on this fact: God's light came into the world, but people loved the darkness more than the light, for their actions were evil. All who do evil hate the light and refuse to go near it for fear their sins will be exposed."
(John 3:19-20 NLT)

MY TESTIMONY

Some people believe I am not worthy of God's calling on my life, not knowing I serve God privately and publicly. I believe I am fit for whatever God has for my life. I am not the same person I used to be, so whoever people knew me as when I was living in sin before I fully surrendered my life to Christ, is not the person I am today. I do not know that person anymore. Leading by example is challenging, but I have chosen to rely on God's strength. I cannot water down who God is calling me to be so that I can please this world. I did that long enough. I ran from my calling for a long time. Now, I do not run from it, I embrace it.

It does not matter if man says we are not qualified for something if God qualifies us. When God calls us, He will prepare and equip us with everything we need for the call. Some people might be mad that it is you, but they have to take that up with God. They might think that if they do not support you, it will hinder you from progressing. They will block their blessings, trying to block what God is doing in your life. We must stay the course and let God lead us, no matter what.

When God called me to serve Him, I knew it would come with obedience, sacrifice, and changing my life. I knew it would not be easy, and there would be things I might not want to give up, but I also knew that I wanted to honor and please God above everything else. I had no idea how or when it would happen, but I was confident that God would change me. God has changed me, healed me, and renewed me. Living for God means understanding that there are consequences for disregarding His word. I do not want the consequences that come with disobeying God.

I experienced the outcome, and I experienced all the pain that comes with living in sin. I do not want to experience it again. Living and doing things based on my fleshly desires showed me a life I no longer desired. I did things my way, but eventually, I realized the importance of doing things God's way. I want to honor God with my heart, mind, words, and body. So, I decided I wanted my private life to be blemish and spot-free. It is not about being perfect. But we should strive for perfection because God says, in His word, *"that we should be perfect as our Father in Heaven is perfect.*" We make so many excuses for our sins; I was that person, but there is no excuse, and I understand that, so I do not make any. I had to give up many things throughout this journey. I had to forgive others. I had to accept responsibility for my actions and seek repentance.

"Therefore you shall be perfect, just as your Father in heaven is perfect."
(Matthew 5:48 NKJV)

I choose not to curse, drink, smoke, watch porn, masturbate, or engage in fornication. In 2016, during my divorce, I decided to practice abstinence and honor God with my body. Now, over seven years later, I am still abstinent. It has not been easy. It has had its ups and downs, but I know that serving God is never in vain. There were occasions when I participated in gossip. I had to repent, and when people want to gossip about someone, it rubs me the wrong way. I have no interest in being a part of it. I try to avoid it at all costs. Every day, I make an effort to choose God. I do not want the things of this world, and I will let it all go to honor God.

"Get rid of your sins, and leave all iniquity behind you."
(Job 11:14 NLT)

"Flee sexual immorality. Every sin that a man does is outside the body, but he who commits sexual immorality sins against his own body. Or do you not know that your body is the temple of the Holy Spirit who is in you, whom you have from God, and you are not your own? For you were bought at a price; therefore glorify God in your body and in your spirit, which are God's."
(1 Corinthians 6:18-20 NKJV)

I do not seek praise from the world because I care more about what God thinks about me. I never want to live a double life. I never want to praise the name of God publicly and privately be in all types of sin. I understand that it is wrong and that is not what I want in my life. When I am wrong, God corrects me, and I repent. I do not make excuses because right is right, and wrong is wrong. When you choose to live a life that truly honors God, your life will make others uncomfortable. Not only will it make them uncomfortable, but it will also offend them. *But we cannot please this world. We must choose God above everything else.*

78

I have had people make fun of me for how I choose to live my life. Many people do not think you can have a fun and fulfilling life when living for Christ because you have to give up certain worldly pleasures. I do not miss the pain, anxiety, depression, trauma, heartbreak, and spiritual warfare that come with living in sin. All the pleasure that people brag about is temporary. None of it is worth it. It is not worth my peace, time, relationships, or eternity.

When God opens your eyes, you view the world differently and understand that *nothing is more important than your relationship with God.* You know that no man or woman is worth you falling into sexual sin for. We do not understand that when we claim to love and serve God, we must show it with our actions. *When you love and serve God, you choose to obey His word.* If a person is aligned with God, they will not lead me away from Him. They will not lead me into sexual sin, and they will not lead me into anything that is against God's word. Anything that we put above God is *idolatry,* whether that is a person, a place, or a thing. So, if you are in a relationship and both of you claim to love and serve God, but you guys are in fornication, you guys are not aligned with God. Not only are you sinning against God, but you are also leading someone else into sexual sin. So, the consequences are going to be worse.

I have been in sexual sin, and I know it is not worth it. I have had to repent. I did not just have to repent, but I also had to turn away from the sin. I know this chapter may come with a lot of conviction, but allow that conviction to lead you to Christ. Allow it to lead you to repentance and help you turn away from your sins. It is difficult, but it can be done with God's strength, power, and grace. You will never regret choosing to honor God and being obedient to His word.

"No temptation has overtaken you except such as is common to man; but God is faithful, who will not allow you to be tempted beyond what you are able, but with the temptation will also make the way of escape, that you may be able to bear it."
(I Corinthians 10:13 NKJV)

Take a few minutes to reflect and write down these things:

1. Write down things you know you are doing privately that are against God's word.
   <u>Renounce and repent for them.</u>

2. Write down scriptures that talk about the sins that you are committing privately.
   <u>When we water down sin, it is easier for us to sin against God, but when we read the word, we see sin for what it is.</u>

Example: We call certain things pleasure, but the Bible calls it sin. We call it cheating, but the Bible calls it adultery.

PRAYER

Dear Heavenly Father,

I repent for my sins and for the sins of my ancestors when it comes to my private life. I renounce and rebuke any evil covenants and curses that were formed due to living a life full of deception. We have not truly been honoring you with our lives. We have been hypocrites. We have publicly lived one way and privately lived another way.

We have tried to deceive you and others. We have used your name in vain and took your grace for granted. We have lived a life full of lies and rebellion. We have led your flock astray because of our selfish desires. We have tried to steal your glory and praise. We have let greed and pride blind us.

We have chosen the world over you. We have let lust, perversion, and sexual sin destroy our lives. We have let drugs, alcohol, and other vices lead us away from you. We have let things of this world become idols in our lives. We have lacked self-control and have lived a double life. Your word says in *James* 1:8 *KJV* that *a double-minded man is unstable in all his ways.* I come out of agreement with the spirit of double-mindedness. Lord, help me no longer be double-minded.

I ask for your forgiveness and mercy upon my bloodline. I repent for deception, double-mindedness, disobedience, pride, all sexual sin, selfishness, and dishonor. I repent for being a hypocrite and for leading others astray by how I live my life. I have not been living according to your word, and I ask for your forgiveness. I repent for taking your grace for granted. Help me never take your grace or mercy for granted.

Help me to truly be a light and not a hypocrite. I want to honor you in every area of my life. I no longer want to be in willing sin. I repent for making excuses for my sin. I want to serve you in spirit and in truth. Lord, restore me from the inside out.

Remove the spirit of deception and disobedience from my life. Let me see sin the way you see sin, so I no longer water down my sin. I have let Satan have authority in my life by being disobedient to your word. I command that disobedience no longer has authority in my life. I declare I will no longer be in willing sin. I declare I will no longer publicly praise your name and privately serve Satan.

Lord, please remove all residue of disobedience, dishonor, and rebellion from my life. Cancel all demonic assignments on my life because of disobedience and deception. I forgive myself for all the lies and deceit. I forgive myself for putting my fleshly desires above your word. From this day forward, I will try to live a life that honors you publicly and privately.

If I fall short, God, please cover me with your grace. I am ready to truly walk the walk. I want to live a life of obedience. I ask that you cover my bloodline with the blood of Jesus and let the blood of Jesus answer on our behalf against every attack of the enemy. Thank you for your forgiveness, grace, and mercy. In the name of Jesus Christ, Amen.

8

SPIRITUAL WARFARE

We are spiritual beings, so spiritual warfare is enviable. We look at the world from a carnal aspect, but everything is spiritual. *We will experience spiritual warfare throughout our lives,* even if we do not know that we are experiencing it. Relationships, music, sex, drugs, things we watch, and what we listen to all matter. They all affect our lives and choices.

When we are born, we are born into an imperfect world, and we are born imperfect people. Satan tries to attack us spiritually when we are young because we do not know any better. It is easy for us to be deceived, manipulated, and led astray. So, as we grow, we are being attacked spiritually, and we do not even know it. The goal is for Satan to attack us spiritually to destroy us because it will lead us to lose faith in God, and over time, we might even stop believing in God because of all the bad things we experienced. The Bible talks about how we will experience things, but God has overcome the world.

"For though we walk in the flesh, we do not war according to the flesh."
(II Corinthians 10:3 NKJV)

"I have told you all this so that you may have peace in me. Here on earth

you will have many trials and sorrows. But take heart, because I have overcome the world."
(John 16:33 NLT)

Living for God does not eliminate all spiritual warfare. It blocks some spiritual warfare, but we will still experience some form of spiritual warfare. When we have a relationship with God, He prepares and equips us to endure and overcome the spiritual attacks on our lives. Our foundation will not be broken when it is built on God. If we want to win against the attacks of the enemy, we must keep God as the center of our lives. *When we build with God as the foundation, what we build will stand.* It will not fall, it will not break, and it will not be overcome. *With God, we can withstand any and every attack on our lives.*

"Therefore whoever hears these sayings of Mine, and does them, I will liken him to a wise man who built his house on the rock: and the rain descended, the floods came, and the winds blew and beat on that house; and it did not fall, for it was founded on the rock. "But everyone who hears these sayings of Mine, and does not do them, will be like a foolish man who built his house on the sand: and the rain descended, the floods came, and the winds blew and beat on that house; and it fell. And great was its fall."
(Matthew 7:24-27 NKJV)

One of the main spiritual attacks we experience is temptation. We are tempted daily to sin against God and give into our fleshly desires, but God provides us with the necessary tools to overcome the desires of our flesh When we give into our flesh, we open up the door for more spiritual attacks. When we kill the flesh, we overcome the attacks. By overcoming, we strengthen our spirit and become better equipped to resist future attacks. That is why we have to be alert and on guard at all times against attacks of the enemy.

"Be sober, be vigilant; because your adversary the devil walks about like a roaring lion, seeking whom he may devour."
(I Peter 5:8 NKJV)

"Let no one say when he is tempted, "I am tempted by God"; for God cannot be tempted by evil, nor does He Himself tempt anyone. But each one is tempted when he is drawn away by his own desires and enticed. Then, when

desire has conceived, it gives birth to sin; and sin, when it is full-grown, brings forth death."
(James 1:13-15 NKJV)

We think we are fighting against people, but we are fighting against demonic spirits. The Bible says that *we do not wrestle against flesh and blood but against the principalities of darkness.* We will always be defeated if we do not know what we are fighting against and how to fight. We need the word, which must be planted in our hearts. We need wisdom to make wise choices, we need discernment to know right from wrong, and we need the ability to discern spirits so that we cannot be deceived by who someone appears to be. We must go to war in prayer. Satan wants us to be misguided and fight each other instead of going to God's word.

"Put on all of God's armor so that you will be able to stand firm against all strategies of the devil. For we are not fighting against flesh-and-blood enemies, but against evil rulers and authorities of the unseen world, against mighty powers in this dark world, and against evil spirits in the heavenly places. Therefore, put on every piece of God's armor so you will be able to resist the enemy in the time of evil. Then after the battle you will still be standing firm. Stand your ground, putting on the belt of truth and the body armor of God's righteousness. For shoes, put on the peace that comes from the Good News so that you will be fully prepared. In addition to all of these, hold up the shield of faith to stop the fiery arrows of the devil. Put on salvation as your helmet, and take the sword of the Spirit, which is the word of God. Pray in the Spirit at all times and on every occasion. Stay alert and be persistent in your prayers for all believers everywhere."
(Ephesians 6: 11-18 NLT)

We can and will overcome the spiritual attacks on our lives with the proper resources. It's time for us to *fight every battle with God.* We cannot afford to fight without the whole armor of God. We cannot afford to fight people when this is a spiritual battle. When spiritual warfare comes, fight it with God. He has overcome this world, and with Him, we can too. It's time for us to take what we have been given and go to war as *warriors of Christ.*

MY TESTIMONY

In the past, spiritual attacks left me feeling completely defeated. I would allow fear and my emotions to control how I handled situations. I lacked spiritual wisdom and discernment. I fought against people and let Satan have authority in my life because I chose the flesh over God's word. I lost battle after battle; even when I thought I won in the physical, I lost in the spiritual.

When we are not given the proper tools, we need to fight spiritual warfare, we experience a lot of unnecessary pain, and we make a lot of bad choices. I did not have the tools to fight against the enemy's attacks, so I would continuously be defeated. *God never intended for us to fight any battles without Him.* Now that I know better, I do not fight without God. I seek Him in prayer and put on the armor of God to prepare for battle. We often undermine spiritual attacks because of our carnal way of thinking. Ignoring spiritual warfare does not mean it does not exist. It just means that you cannot fight the spiritual attacks properly or win. Learning how to fight my battles with God completely transformed my life. It came with less worry and less stress.

Since I was a little girl, I always felt like I did not fit in. The way I thought and how I wanted to live my life was different from most people. I was introduced to God at a young age, and that was a blessing because it set the foundation for my life. Anything that had to do with God felt like home to me. I loved going to church and learning about God. I knew I wanted to live a life serving Christ, but I was not truly taught how to do that. It took years for me to give my life to Christ and truly live His way.

I believe the attacks from Satan on my life started while I was in my mother's womb. Satan wanted to destroy me before I was born. He attacked me as a child because he wanted me to lose my trust in God. He wanted my bad experiences to keep me from God's will for my life. For a long time, that was the case, but *what Satan tried to use for evil, God used for my good.*

"You intended to harm me, but God intended it all for good. He brought me to this position so I could save the lives of many people."
(Genesis 50:20 NLT)

One area I experienced spiritual warfare was in self-confidence. It was easy for Satan to attack me in this area because of my speech. I am unsure when it came about, but I developed a stutter as a child. It made me feel inadequate because I was the only person I knew in my family who had it. I let it make me insecure about public speaking and talking to people I did not know. Not only did I have a stutter, but I was also shy.

I remember I used to pray for God to heal me, but it did not happen. I did not understand why He would not heal me, but over time, it improved, and I did not do it as often. I did not know it then, but those things were put in place to block me from what God wanted to do in me. I owned the shyness and the stutter. I let it control my life, and I let it hold me back from a lot of things.

When God wanted to use me, I felt like, *why me?* Why would He want to use me to speak? I felt like if God wanted to use me, why wouldn't He heal me? Fear…I let fear take over. Once again, fear had the front seat in my life. God could not heal me because of fear. As I talked about in Chapter Two, you cannot have faith and fear at the same time. One will also triumph over the other.

I got to a point where I decided I would trust God's plan for my life. I did not want to be in fear because it affected my confidence, self-worth, and purpose, but God… I know that His plans for my life are greater than those I have for myself. He has built up my confidence and self-worth. I went from letting people make me feel small to letting God use me as a vessel. I slept on myself because others slept on me, but *I am coming for everything God has for me.*

Now, God is using the shy girl who was afraid to speak in a room full of people to teach His word, and I am in awe of it. Satan has no authority over my voice or my life. I will not let anything stop me from speaking or teaching the word of God. What God wants me to speak, I will speak. Even when my speech failed me, God never did. *I lack nothing.* I do not need approval from the people of this world, and you should not need their approval either. No matter what area in your life you may feel that you lack, *with God, you lack nothing*, and when He calls you, He will equip you with everything you need to fulfill His will for your life. Trust the process.

December 13, 2023

Journal Entry

I had a revelation that when I was under spiritual attacks, I would panic, and I would be stressed. My body would be on high alert, and I would feel fear. I would allow all those emotions to take over before praying. God showed me I would not trust Him in that moment. I would let the spirit of fear have the front seat. For a long time, fear was a stronghold in my life. I do not allow fear to run my life anymore. As I grow in my walk with Christ, God has been building my spirit, and I feel like my spirit is strong. My spirit is at peace.

Take a few minutes to reflect and write down these things:

1. Write down any spiritual attacks you are experiencing in this season.
   Pray against the attacks on your life.

2. Write down how you have been fighting these spiritual attacks.
   Pray and repent for fighting the wrong way.

Examples: Arguing, fighting, drugs, alcohol, etc.

3. Write down emotions you are allowing to take over.
   Rebuke and pray against the emotions.

Examples: Depression, anxiety, anger, fear, etc.

4. Write down scriptures that will prepare and equip you for spiritual warfare.
   Pray the scriptures over your life.

PRAYER

Dear Heavenly Father,

I repent for my sins and for the sins of my ancestors when it comes to spiritual warfare. I renounce and rebuke any evil covenants and curses that were formed due to not seeking you first during spiritual attacks. I repent for fighting the wrong way. I repent for taking matters into my own hands instead of coming to you. I have tried to use things of this world to help fix my feelings and emotions during spiritual attacks. I repent for my ignorance. I repent for falling into temptation when it was presented to me.

I repent for not overcoming the desires of my flesh. I repent for choosing my flesh above your word. I know we do not fight against flesh and blood, so I repent for fighting against flesh and blood. I will no longer fight without you. I want to fight according to your word. I know I will never win any spiritual battle without you.

You are the source. Your word is what I need to get wisdom, and your armor is what I need to win against the attacks of the enemy. My flesh has no authority over my life, and it will no longer be a stumbling block in my life. *I declare your full armor over my life: the belt of truth, the breastplate of righteousness, the gospel of peace, the shield of faith, the helmet of salvation, and the sword of the spirit. (Ephesians 6:11-17)* I will no longer let depression, fear, anxiety, or suicidal thoughts take over my life.

When negative feelings come, I will kill them at the root with your word. I choose to fight with you because I know *I will overcome every attack on my life.* Thank you for your wisdom, guidance, discernment, and protection. Thank you for giving me peace in the midst of the storms. Thank you for covering me with the blood of Jesus and for not allowing me to look like what I have been through. In the name of Jesus Christ, Amen.

9

DELIVERANCE

A lot of believers never get delivered from their sins. They serve God for years and never experienced deliverance. They live their life in bondage. Most people think that if you get saved, you are set free. You are not truly set free until you are delivered from your iniquities, transgressions, and sins.

"The righteous cry out, and the Lord hears, And delivers them out of all their troubles."
(Psalms 34:17 NKJV)

Sometimes, we think we are set free from certain sins because we go through periods not falling into that sin, but because we are not delivered at some point, we will fall into that sin again. We will still have those traits, and that spirit will still be in us. When we get delivered, we can overcome the temptation. It will no longer be a stumbling block in our lives. Satan no longer has any authority in that area of our life. His access will be denied.

Satan is always looking for an open door in our lives. Day and night, he accuses us of our sins before God, that is why repentance and deliverance is crucial. When we sin, we give Satan the legal right to destroy our lives. Satan can accuse, but when we repent and receive deliverance, it removes the legal authority he has to access our lives. Then Satan can no longer accuse what God has forgiven; that is why we must know the scriptures because *Satan uses the scriptures as a weapon against us.* We get deceived because we do not know God's word.

Our level of effort must surpass that of Satan. We need to pray daily, repent daily, and seek deliverance often because he is working day and night. In some cases, we may need to seek deliverance from things on our bloodline, such as generational curses and covenants. *Generational curses stay on our bloodline until someone comes as the repair of the breach to break the demonic curses and covenants off our bloodline.*

"Those from among you Shall build the old waste places; You shall raise up the foundations of many generations; And you shall be called the Repairer of the Breach, The Restorer of Streets to Dwell In."
(Isaiah 58:12 NKJV)

Most Christians do not believe that covenants are on our bloodline, and some people think they do not affect us, but they do. They pass down from generation to generation. They destroy our lives and keep us from our blessings. We suffer for years from the curses and covenants on our bloodline because we do not know how to break them. It's time for us to get the knowledge to be delivered and set free.

Demonic spirits come into our lives through open doors from us living in sin. Sin gives Satan the authority to send demonic spirits into our lives. These demonic spirits change us, such as our personality, how we dress, how we live, and how we think. There are all types of demonic spirits. For instance, the Jezebel spirit, a spirit of perversion, a spirit of poverty, a spirit of envy, monitoring spirits, and seducing spirits. When these spirits attach to our spirit, we are bound to them and everything that comes with them. Their job is to destroy our lives, and that is exactly what they do.

For example, when someone has a seducing spirit, they may be a seductress and lead people into temptation and sexual sin. We can have certain spirits in us and not know it; that is why deliverance is so essential, as well as being able to discern spirits. A seducing spirit may even have a seducing walk or talk, and they may do things such as licking their lips in a seducing way. Some health issues are caused by demonic spirits. Many scriptures talk about Jesus doing deliverance on people and it healing them from demonic spirits. In *Matthew*, it talks about how Jesus healed a child who had seizures by casting out the demonic spirit that was in the child.

"Lord, have mercy on my son. He has seizures and suffers terribly. He often falls into the fire or into the water. So I brought him to your disciples, but they couldn't heal him. Jesus said, "You faithless and corrupt people! How long must I be with you? How long must I put up with you? Bring the boy here to me." Then Jesus rebuked the demon in the boy, and it left him. From that moment the boy was well. Afterward the disciples asked Jesus privately, "Why couldn't we cast out that demon?" "You don't have enough faith," Jesus told them. "I tell you the truth, if you had faith even as small as a mustard seed, you could say to this mountain, 'Move from here to there,' and it would move. Nothing would be impossible."
(Matthew 17:15-20 NLT)

Most of the time, we think that the illnesses we experience are normal, but sometimes it's demonic spirits. Some health issues, such as cancer, stroke, and high blood pressure, can be from generational curses on our bloodline. To break these things off of us, we need deliverance. Until we go through deliverance, we will have these demonic spirits attached to us. Even if we serve God, we must still go through deliverance. We must also stay delivered because we do not want the demonic spirits to return. If they return, they will return with more demonic spirits and be even more potent. So, we have to be alert and not allow them access to our lives.

"When an evil spirit leaves a person, it goes into the desert, seeking rest but finding none. Then it says, 'I will return to the person I came from.' So it returns and finds its former home empty, swept, and in order. Then the spirit finds seven other spirits more evil than itself, and they all enter the person and live there. And so that person is worse off than before. That will be the experience of this evil generation."
(Matthew 12:43-45 NLT)

We do not have to suffer from demonic curses or covenants in our lives any longer. *God can and will set us free.* We must choose the freedom that comes with living for Christ. *Our bloodline cannot afford for us not to break free from demonic covenants and curses.* We must get serious about deliverance because it's time for us to be the repairer of the breach.

"When Jesus climbed out of the boat, a man possessed by an evil spirit came out from the tombs to meet him. This man lived in the burial caves and could no longer be restrained, even with a chain. Whenever he was put into chains and shackles—as he often was—he snapped the chains from his wrists and smashed the shackles. No one was strong enough to subdue him. Day and night he wandered among the burial caves and in the hills, howling and cutting himself with sharp stones. When Jesus was still some distance away, the man saw him, ran to meet him, and bowed low before him. With a shriek, he screamed, "Why are you interfering with me, Jesus, Son of the Most High God? In the name of God, I beg you, don't torture me!" For Jesus had already said to the spirit, "Come out of the man, you evil spirit." Then Jesus demanded, "What is your name?" And he replied, "My name is Legion, because there are many of us inside this man." Then the evil spirits begged him again and again not to send them to some distant place. There happened to be a large herd of pigs feeding on the hillside nearby. "Send us into those pigs," the spirits begged. "Let us enter them." So Jesus gave them permission. The evil spirits came out of the man and entered the pigs, and the entire herd of about 2,000 pigs plunged down the steep hillside into the lake and drowned in the water. A crowd soon gathered around Jesus, and they saw the man who had been possessed by the legion of demons. He was sitting there fully clothed and perfectly sane, and they were all afraid. Then those who had seen what happened told the others about the demon-possessed man and the pigs."
(*Mark 5:2-13, 15-16 NLT*)

MY TESTIMONY

I knew little about deliverance. I heard of it and saw a few videos here and there, but overall deliverance looked kind of weird to me. In August 2023, I read a book called Deliverance from Demonic Covenants and Curses by *Reverend James A. Solomon.* Reading that book changed my viewpoint about deliverance. It helped me understand why deliverance was so important.

I knew I had generational curses on my bloodline, but I did not know how to break them. That book and the Bible gave me the tools to do self-deliverance. After I went through self-deliverance, I felt like a new person. The fire that I had been seeking from God was restored. Since August 2023, my life has not been the same. Spiritually, I feel stronger. I started my faith-based YouTube channel in August 2023. God put it on my heart in 2020, but I allowed fear to have me in disobedience. I did not feel fit for the call. When I first began to film, I would be super nervous, but over time, I could feel the Holy Spirit take over, and my confidence grew.

I started writing this book in October 2023. God put it on my heart to do a book in 2020, but I did not write it. I had to repent for being disobedient. The reason I did not do it did not matter because I was still in disobedience. If I had not gone through deliverance, I would not have written this book or started my YouTube channel. I also believe that I would not have been able to complete the things that God has led me to do within a short period.

Now, I am learning new things when it comes to the Bible. I am learning more about God's order and the importance of being obedient to what God is telling me to do. Deliverance has set me free from wallowing in sin. When we go through deliverance, we are being set free from demonic spirits, covenants, and curses that have been destroying our lives. We must seek God and let Him lead us to what He wants for our lives. I will continue to seek knowledge from God and apply what I learn because there is *freedom in obedience.*

There are blessings that come with obedience.
- Lakeisha Goudy

"But it shall come to pass, if you do not obey the voice of the Lord your God, to observe carefully all His commandments and His statutes which I command you today, that all these curses will come upon you and overtake you:"
(Deuteronomy 28:15 NKJV)

Take a few minutes to reflect and write down these things:

1. Write down generational curses that are on your bloodline. (Be specific)
    <u>Pray, renounce, and rebuke the curses that are on your bloodline.</u>

Examples: poverty, drugs, prison, premature death, cancer, divorce, children out of wedlock, etc.

2. Write down the demonic covenants you have made.
    <u>Pray and repent for them. (come out of agreement with them)</u>

Examples: blood covenants, fornication, abortion, etc.

3. Write down scriptures that talk about breaking generational curses.
    <u>Pray the scriptures over your life.</u>

PRAYER

Dear Heavenly Father,

I repent for my sins and for the sins of my ancestors. I renounce, denounce, and rebuke all evil covenants and curses that were formed because of our sins. I repent for our disobedience and dishonor. I repent for our ignorance and pride. Now that I know better, I want to do better. I repent for choosing temporary pleasure and for my lack of self-control. I pray you help me have self-control in every area of my life.

I no longer want to live in bondage. I want to be set free. Help me seek you above all things. I surrender my life to you. I surrender my plans to you. I want what you want for my life. I ask for your healing, deliverance, and freedom. Living for you is not easy, but I know that with you, I can do all things. Your word says you have overcome this world, and I can, too.

I pray that as I get delivered from all demonic covenants and curses the blood of Jesus Christ answers on my behalf. I pray against all attacks of the enemy on my life. I pray no weapon formed against me shall prosper and that every voice that rises against me in unrighteous judgment will be condemned. Lord, redeem and restore everything the enemy has stolen from me.

I ask for your forgiveness, mercy, and grace upon my bloodline. Renew my heart, mind, spirit, and body from the inside out. I declare I am a new creation; my past does not define me. Thank you for your wisdom, guidance, discernment, and protection. Thank you for giving me the knowledge I need to make better choices. Thank you for giving me peace in the midst of trials and tribulations. In the name of Jesus Christ, Amen.

"These things I have spoken to you, that in Me you may have peace. In the world you will have tribulation; but be of good cheer, I have overcome the world."
(John 16:33 NKJV)

Deliverance

10

ALL THINGS NEW

This chapter is called *All Things New* because God makes *All Things New*. He makes everything new in our hearts, spirits, thoughts, and minds. He transforms us from the inside out and gives us a clean slate. How does it feel to start fresh with a clean slate? God's goodness is shown through forgiving our sins and giving us a new beginning. I truly understand what the Bible means when it says *where the spirit of the Lord is, there is freedom*. I now understand what that means because wherever God is, there is freedom because He covers, guides, protects, and loves us. Knowing the truth sets us free, and we no longer have to live in bondage.

"For the Lord is the Spirit, and wherever the Spirit of the Lord is, there is freedom."
(2 Corinthians 3:17 NLT)

If you want God to make everything new in your life and restore the things Satan took from you, He will. God will restore, and He will give back more than you lost. It all starts with your faith and trusting God because He has a purpose for your life. That purpose will be fulfilled when you are aligned with His word. Being aligned with the word of God includes forgiving those who have trespassed against you, forgiving yourself for things you have done, and repenting for your sins. Accountability and correction are crucial when it comes to your walk with God.

Things will happen, and sometimes you will make mistakes, but you must always ensure you diligently seek *God.* Make sure you live according to God's word in private and public. Never think that you can fool God because you cannot. You must do the work behind the scenes when no one is watching. Spiritual warfare will happen, but you can endure and overcome every attack on your life with God.

Last but not least, deliverance is vital on your walk because you need to be set free from all the demonic spirits, covenants, and curses in your life. If you stay the course, you will see it is all worth it. I hope you choose faith over fear, love over hate, healing over pain, repentance over pride, wisdom over ignorance, and obedience over disobedience. *Putting your trust in God will never be in vain.*

God can and will heal and redeem you, no matter what you have been through. You will experience many things in life, but God will give you hope, love, peace, joy, and much more. God is the source of *all things.* You need Him in every area of your life. It's time to walk in all God has called you to be. It's time for you to walk in the purpose God has for your life, help the people God wants you to help, and create what God wants you to create. Lives are on the line, and God is calling you to help change lives. It's time for you to walk into your new season of *All Things New.*

"Do not remember the former things, Nor consider the things of old. Behold, I will do a new thing, Now it shall spring forth; Shall you not know it? I will make a road in the wilderness And rivers in the desert."
(Isaiah 43:18-19)

"And God will wipe away every tear from their eyes; there shall be no more death, nor sorrow, nor crying. There shall be no more pain, for the former things have passed away." Then He who sat on the throne said, "Behold, I make all things new." And He said to me, "Write, for these words are true and faithful."
(Revelation 21:4-5)

MY TESTIMONY

This book is my testimony for this chapter because it was created in my season of *All Thing New*. Not only is God making All Things New in my life, but He has been using me in ways I never thought He would. I do not know what all God has in store for me, but I know it is more than I can imagine. When I started writing this chapter, I got emotional because God has been taking all the broken parts of me and making them new.

If God can use me, He can use you, too. I have been through a lot in life, and I have made a lot of mistakes, but *God still chose me*. I always get emotional thinking about it because God is so good. He has been good to me even when I did not deserve it. When I went my way and was living in sin, God welcomed me with open arms. He gave me grace, but He also corrected me because He did not want me to stay the same. I had to change and be better. I wanted to change and be a better person. *I was never content living a life that was not pleasing to God,* and I never had peace living in sin.

I cannot imagine my life without God. I do not know where I would be today without Him; He is my rock, my redeemer, my healer, my father, my everything. I am not where I want to be, but I am far from who I used to be. The person I was is long gone, and I do not know that person anymore. Returning to my old life is out of the question because my heart has been completely renewed. I do not even have a taste for my old life because God has changed my life for the better. I am truly a new creation and *God has done a new thing in my life*. He has done so much for me, and I am forever grateful. I hope this book helps lead you closer to Christ and encourages you on your walk with God. Behold, He is making *All Things New!*

"Therefore, if anyone is in Christ, he is a new creation; old things have passed away; behold, all things have become new."
(II Corinthians 5:17 NKJV)

June 13, 2021
Journal Entry

Five years ago, I was going through a horrible divorce, and I was so broken. I was tired of being treated less than I deserved, and I knew I wanted to give my kids a better life. Deep down, I knew I deserved better, but I did not know how to get there. I remember I used to cry myself to sleep in my marriage, and now I cry tears of joy. I am not where I want to be, but I am far from who I used to be. I knew there were a lot of things I needed to change.

I remember praying and asking God to take the pain away because heartbreak is no joke. I remember hearing God say, " *I will take care of you and your kids. I am going to make sure you guys have everything you need."* So, I took a leap of faith and filed for divorce. I had no money saved; I had to move out of my place, my kids and I had to stay with other people, I did not have a car, and I did not even have my license because I did not know how to drive. (I had a fear of car accidents.)

Stepping out on faith has been one of the best things I have ever done because not only did God restore what I lost, but He gave me so much more. This journey has not been easy because I had to die to myself a lot, and it did not feel good. (This is a daily thing I still have to do.) I had to forgive people who hurt me, and I had to forgive myself for the poor choices I have made in my life. I still make mistakes, but I do not stay there. Overall, I am so proud of the woman I am becoming because no matter what obstacles come my way, I never give up.

It took years to get here, and if people could see the work, I do behind the scenes, they would understand why I am so proud of myself. I wake up thankful every single day, and I wake up knowing I am loved. When my kids grow up, I want them to see a strong, God-fearing woman who knows her worth. When I say I am blessed, it's more about the inner things. Everything that was meant to break me, God used for my good. I have been able to give my kids a better life.

I am writing this on the plane ride home from Mexico, crying happy tears. *I do not have to settle anymore in any area of my life.* I just feel *free* from the weight of the world. I barely worry about things anymore because I trust God. I am in a happy place in my life.

Take a few minutes to reflect and write down these things:

1. Write down prayers you are believing for God to answer. (Be specific)

2. Write down what you are thankful for.
   Thank God for all He has done in your life.

3. Write down scriptures that are promises from God that align with what you are praying and believing for.
   Pray the scriptures over your life.

PRAYER

Dear Heavenly Father,

Thank you for teaching me your ways. Thank you for shielding me from the unknown. Thank you for your love, grace, and mercy. Thank you for your peace. Thank you for your guidance. Thank you for helping me understand your word.

I appreciate everything you have done in my life. Thank you for blessing me with my family, friends, and all the people you have brought into my life. Thank you for removing the wrong people from my life. Thank you for turning my *lessons into blessings*. Thank you for giving me a healthy mind, body, and spirit. Thank you for instilling a purpose in me.

Thank you for my faith, healing, and ability to forgive others. Thank you for granting me forgiveness for my sins. Thank you for granting me the chance to seek forgiveness and amend my past mistakes. Thank you for your wisdom and discernment. Thank you for giving me the ability to discern spirits. Thank you for your accountability and correction.

Thank you for showing me how to live righteously in private and in public. Thank you for protecting me during spiritual warfare and for helping me overcome it all. Thank you for rescuing me from my sinful ways and wrongdoings. Thank you for showering me with your blessings. Thank you for leaving the *ninety-nine* to get me the *one*. Thank you for making *All Things New* in my life. I declare that in this new season, I will walk in the freedom and peace you have given me. In the name of Jesus Christ, Amen

ABOUT THE AUTHOR

Lakeisha Goudy is a first-time author. She is also a Life Coach and runs a YouTube channel focused on teaching the word of God through faith. She is a proud mother of three and a dog mom. Lakeisha has a passion for helping others. She finds pleasure in devoting time to God and her family. In addition, she takes pleasure in praying, serving the community, dancing, skating, and traveling. She resides in Sacramento, California.

Get Connected:

YouTube: Lakeisha Goudy

Instagram: lakeishagoudy

Main Instagram: Goudy1

TikTok: @lakeishagoudy

ABOUT THE AUTHOR BY FAMILY

"Lakeisha, my second oldest sister, is caring. She took me in as a kid and raised me when she was only nineteen. She is a phenomenal mother. She knows her worth, and because of this, she never settles. She is beautiful on the inside and out."
- *Larissa*

"My mom, Lakeisha, is a hard worker. She is smart, and she is devoted to God."
-*De'jon*

"My mom, Lakeisha, is kind to everyone that she meets. She takes care of everyone. She loves to help people in need. She will always be there for you. She has been a really good mom and helps me with many things. I can always count on her to be there for me."
- *Cameryn*

"My mom, Lakeisha, is kind. She is pretty, and everyone is always trying to talk to her. She puts everyone before herself. She is very smart. She thinks she can dance. She likes working out. She is a Christian. I would want people to know these things about my amazing mom."
- *Cayden*